The Baseball Starter

The Baseball Starter

A Handbook for Coaching Children and Teens

W. George Scarlett, Gregory Chertok,
Jacob L. Lipton *and* Erik S. Johanson

Foreword by Sol Gittleman

McFarland & Company, Inc., Publishers
Jefferson, North Carolina, and London

Unless otherwise credited all photographs are by Melody Komyerov

LIBRARY OF CONGRESS ONLINE CATALOG DATA

Scarlett, W. George.
The baseball starter : a handbook for coaching children and teens / W. George Scarlett, Gregory Chertok, Jacob L. Lipton and Erik S. Johanson ; foreword by Sol Gittleman.
p.   cm.
Includes bibliographical references and index.

ISBN 978-0-7864-3858-7
softcover : 50# alkaline paper ∞

1. Baseball for children — Coaching — Handbooks, manuals, etc.
GV880.4.B37   2010   796.357'62 — dc22   2009039620

British Library cataloguing data are available

Front cover photograph by Melody Komyerov

Manufactured in the United States of America

McFarland & Company, Inc., Publishers
Box 611, Jefferson, North Carolina 28640
www.mcfarlandpub.com

Table of Contents

Acknowledgments

This book was several years in the making, and a good many people contributed. As even a brief glance will indicate, Melody Komyerov's photographs provide the book with wonderful visuals. We are grateful for her work. We are also grateful for John Della Volpe's organizing the players who were photographed for this book and for the skill and patience of the players themselves: Andrew Della Volpe, Christopher Giles, Wyatt Powell, Drew Coash, and Seamus Vahey.

We are grateful too for the work that Cara Hohvanessian, Alex Prewitt, and Christina Palermo put into helping draft chapters and provide examples. The book would not have turned out as it did without their contributions.

During the project's first year, when it was developing along different lines (toward producing an electronic book), a number of people contributed in a variety of ways. While the project took a different direction in its second year, that first year laid the foundation. We are particularly grateful for the support and input provided then by Elizabeth Pufall, George Forman, Jesse Pearlman, David Schloss, C.J. Horvath, Charles Fitzpatrick, and Evan Scarlett.

Finally, we would like to thank coach John Casey for his support from the beginning, for his giving batting instructions to an over-the-hill baseball player, the lead author, and for his ongoing enthusiasm for this project.

Foreword
by Sol Gittleman

We have come a long way in this country since I told my father right after the 1941 World Series that I wanted to play shortstop for the New York Yankees when Phil Rizzuto was finished. That was the dream of a seven-year-old boy who somehow knew that he would not grow much taller, and identified emotionally with the diminutive Yankee shortstop. My father was my first and perhaps best coach. He was a kind, patient mentor who loved baseball as only an immigrant could and wanted his son to love it too. He took me to Yankee Stadium, taught me how to throw a baseball, and told me how to watch a game, how each hitter and fielder performed. "See where they throw the ball. Every outfielder tries to hit the infielder in the chest. Aim for the chest when you are throwing. If it's a relay, make sure they can turn easily in the right direction. Aim for the chest and the glove." I would go to sleep muttering, "Aim for the chest," and see myself taking relays from the outfield and turning effortlessly to make a perfect pivot and throw a perfect strike to the catcher, just in time to nip the runner at home plate.

It was a wonderful dream, and it stayed with me all through the Build Better Boys leagues, American Legion ball, and college ball. I taught my son Thomas, "Aim for the chest, and make the pivot easy for the fielder."

Now, I am a grandfather and have observed a half-century of enormous growth in youth baseball, from the Little League championships in Williamsport, Pennsylvania, to the collegiate World Series in Omaha, Nebraska. Over that period, I have been waiting for a coach as good as my father, or at least a book to help other coaches. Finally, I have found one.

More than anything else in life, I want my six-year-old grandson Frank (named after my father) to love baseball, but that won't happen until his coach — a very successful hedge fund manager — stops trying to teach him the game the way *he* was taught it. So, what do I hear coming from this suburban version of John McGraw? "It's just a little cut. *Real* ballplayers learn to rub it in the dirt.... It's *supposed* to hurt! Pain is part of the game.... Pay attention out there! You're

1

not Ferdinand the Bull, stop smelling the flowers if you want to be a ballplayer.... Keep your eyes open, keep the chatter coming. Let's hear the noise from that infield! Don't just stand around, do something.... When you stand at the plate, look like a hitter.... No, no, don't throw like a girl!" He might be able to organize a portfolio of stocks, but when it comes to putting together a pleasant and effective practice for a dozen T-ballers, all the coach has working for him is his willingness to show up and his own experience two decades earlier as a player. The man is intelligent. But it takes more to be a great coach of children.

My grandson is only a few years away from Little League. What frightens me is the thought that by the time he gets there, he will have turned away from baseball. Coaches who understand the needs of children and who are not trying to replicate their own athletic careers in some fantasy are in desperately short supply. There are uncountable numbers of parents and grandparents who have watched a practice session or game with their children and bit their lips in pain and agony. The ideal situation, expressed in passing in this text, is not about to happen: "It would help if each coach were a professional teacher." Since there is no hope for this miracle to occur, why not provide a manual for the thousands of amateur coaches who volunteer to work with our children right through adolescence?

W. George Scarlett and his colleagues have produced a book to remedy many of these problems and to aid coaches of children and young adolescents, well-intended adults who simply do not know any better. Dumbing down for children is not the answer. Finding a suitable vocabulary of instruction appropriate for children and then translating that language into intelligent action is what Scarlett is seeking.

This is not a pablum approach that emphasizes the non-competitive aspect of baseball. The idea is to *win!* But winning can be fun, and losing while playing the game with skill is not the worst thing in the world. Yes, the fundamental premise is laid out with transparent candor: *everyone* should be involved, regardless of skill level. This is not the Vince Lombardi School of Winning Is Everything. It is not easy for a coach and his staff to be as competitive as possible on the field, and at the same time keep in sight the goal of children's involvement in the enterprise. Nobody said coaching was supposed to be easy.

Here, at last, is a transparent handbook for those coaches who mistakenly think they either know everything, or believe they don't know enough. The visuals are perfect complements to the text. I can't wait to give this as a gift!

The only person who would not need one was my father.

Sol Gittleman is the former provost of Tufts University and author of *Reynolds, Raschi and Lopat: New York's Big Three and the Great Yankee Dynasty of 1949–1953* (McFarland, 2007).

Preface

To coach baseball is to teach baseball. This may sound simple, but it isn't. Usually, it takes years of training and additional years of actual teaching for a professional teacher to teach well. We should all keep this in mind when coaching youth baseball. Our own experience playing baseball — even if that means we played baseball up through college — is not likely to make us qualified to teach youth baseball, which is why we have written this book.

We have written this book for three main reasons. First, from close observation, we know that most youth baseball coaches have a lot to learn about the proper ways to play baseball. A visit to almost any Little League game will show what we mean. In youth baseball games, coaches yell out instructions that indicate they do not fully understand the basics of how to play the game. The instructions are either too vague or too general ("Watch the ball," "Swing hard," "Throw strikes") or they are just plain wrong. As a result, children don't learn — and when they don't learn, they have a less than satisfying experience playing baseball.

Our second reason for writing this book is centered on the fact that most books and films on coaching youth baseball are geared for coaching adolescents. For those who are coaching children, these books and films leave it to the reader or viewer to translate downward; that is, translate the complex explanations that work for adolescents so as to make them work for children.

However, since the process of translating downward is complex and subtle and since most readers and viewers are not professional teachers, these books and films are inadequate as guides to coaching children. In this book, we will be giving two levels of explanation to chose from — one for coaching older players (roughly, players twelve and older), and one for coaching younger players (roughly, players younger than twelve).

Obviously age does not always predict a player's skill level or ability. But generally, players younger than twelve have a difficult time considering more than one relationship simultaneously. For example, it is hard for younger players to simultaneously consider both the stride (stepping forward) and the load (bringing hands back and up) when hitting, and so, for at least some younger players, we suggest simplifying by eliminating the stride. This simplifying process is meant to lay a foundation for younger players, a foundation they can build on as they mature. It is not a process that teaches bad habits.

Our third reason for writing this book is to help make youth baseball more satisfying for children — so satisfying, in fact, that they develop a real love for the game. We believe that when it comes to youth baseball, the primary aim of coaches should be helping players develop a love for the game by teaching them how to play the game well. Nothing breeds satisfaction and a love for the game like playing the game well.

One further comment about coaching as teaching: the foundation of all teaching is knowing how to maintain positive relationships. If a coach cannot relate to children positively and support positive relationships between children, the children won't learn much. Moreover, they won't develop a love for the game. Later in the book, we will have more to say about how coaches can keep relationships positive, especially when things go wrong. For now, it is enough to keep in mind that knowing how to remain positive is something all coaches need to learn.

Introduction

This book will help you learn how to coach youth baseball. But do you really need to learn more than you already know? Your answer will depend on your main goal. If your main goal is simply for players to have fun, then maybe you don't need to learn more — or at least not much more. If, though, your main goal is to develop players' skills and field a competitive team, then you probably do need to learn more. After all, baseball is complex, and teaching baseball to children presents special challenges.

However, we think you need to learn more in order to achieve a different and better goal, namely that of helping children develop a love for baseball. Why do we think this is a better goal? Because baseball means something different for today's youth than it likely did for you, just as it meant something different for you as a youth than it did for your parents. Much of this difference in meaning has to do with changes in unsupervised play in general and backyard sports in particular.

Backyard Baseball

Organized youth baseball has been around for many years, even longer than Little League, which began in 1939. However, for most of its history, organized youth baseball took a back seat to backyard baseball.* This was fine for children, because it was while playing backyard baseball and not so much while playing organized baseball that previous generations of children fell in love with the game.

Why this was the case becomes evident when you look at how backyard baseball was played. Here is an excerpt from Edward Devereux's (1978) well-known essay explaining backyard baseball while also extolling its virtues:

*As the term is generally used, backyard sports are played anywhere and everywhere — including city streets. Alternative terms are pickup and sandlot. Whatever the term, the reference is to informal, child-run games that often simulate aspects of organized team sports such as baseball.

We learned a lot of other kinds of things which are probably more important for children between the ages of eight and twelve. Precisely because there was no official rule book and no adult or even other child designated as rule enforcer, we somehow had to improvise the whole thing; this entailed endless hassles about whether a ball was fair or foul, whether a runner was safe or out, or more generally, simply about what was fair. We gradually learned to understand the invisible boundary conditions of our relationships to each other. Don't be a poor sport or the other kids won't want you to play with them. Don't push your point so hard that the kid with the only catcher's mitt will quit the game. Pitch a bit more gently to the littler kids so they can have some fun, too; besides, you realize that you must keep them in the game because numbers are important. Learn how to get a game started and somehow keep it going, as long as the fun lasts. How to pace it. When to quit for a while to get a round of cokes or just to sit under a tree for a bit. How to recognize the subtle boundaries indicating that the game is really over — not an easy thing, since there are no innings, no winners or losers — and slide over into some other activity ... mostly on to the endless variety of other games, pastimes, and interests which could so engage a young boy on a summer afternoon or evening [p. 122].

Whatever the virtues of backyard baseball, it is clear why backyard baseball led children to love baseball. In backyard baseball, children were in charge. More important, backyard baseball was totally devoted to being with friends, being active, and having fun. While we may claim this is how it is with organized youth baseball, the truth is otherwise because so many coaches put winning ahead of children being with friends, being active, and having fun (Coakley, 1998).

In addition to helping children develop a love for baseball, backyard baseball also helped children develop real skills. Consider the example of the Dominican Republic where the backyard game of *vitilla*, a variant of baseball, is played throughout the country. Equipped with just a broomstick and bottle cap, Dominican children take to the streets and play *vitilla* whenever and wherever they can. Imagine what hitting a curving bottle cap with a thin broomstick can do to prepare children to hit a baseball with a bat. No wonder the Dominican Republic develops so many great ballplayers.

The main thing about backyard baseball was that the children were in charge. When it was time to choose up teams, there were agreed upon methods, such as rocks-scissors-and-paper and team captains using a special method of gripping a bat to see who selects first. Whatever the method used, the result was always the same: teams of friends divided evenly enough to have a competitive game.

Contrast that process with what is happening today. Nowadays, adults do the choosing, often after having "scouted" to find the best players, and usually with only one goal in mind, the goal of winning. The result is often a team of players, some who know one another but most who are not really friends. Only

Children playing *vitilla* in the Dominican Republic (photograph by Stan Grossfeld).

a few adults complain. After all, say the majority, it's important for children to learn to get along with everybody and be able to make new friends.

We don't see it the same way. For children, teams of friends make a great deal of sense. The games matter, but so do the discussions of shared experience that occur outside the games — discussions at school, during car rides, and when visiting each other's homes. How can one discuss shared experience if there is little or none?

The presence of drafts where adults scheme to assemble the "best" team is probably the single most obvious example of what has happened to make youth sports today adult-organized as compared to the child-organized sports in the past. The problem now is that our system for organizing youth sports has become so ingrained that few see the need for a change, despite the many books and articles calling for change. At times, all the books and articles seem to amount to little more than whining in the wilderness. No one really listens — or listens hard enough to want to change.

As evidence for this pessimistic assessment of how things are with youth sports today, consider the book *Managing Little League Baseball* (McIntosh, 2008), a Little League-sanctioned guide, now in its third edition. Here is how the author speaks about the draft:

> Your first important decisions will involve selecting prospects for your team in the player draft. These decisions will affect your team's success and/or frustrations. The player you could have had, but didn't pick, will come back to haunt you..., and the player you did pick, but shouldn't have, will create frustrations.... Just as the professional baseball teams use scouts and do some research prior to their player draft, so should you.... Obviously, you won't get all of the good prospects, since they will be known to the other managers, too, but you owe it to your team to know who they are and to pick them if you have the chance [pp. 2, 3].

Is there anything in this quote that indicates the author cares about the less-skilled players? Is there anything that aims at assembling a team of friends? Finally, is there anything that shows real sensitivity to the needs of children? We don't think there is. In this quote, children aren't children; they are prospects.

Before you say we are being too judgmental and harsh, we need to make it clear that we know the thousands of volunteer coaches who share the perspective expressed in the above quote are good people, people who believe they are providing something good for children. We claim no moral superiority. Furthermore, our claim is not that present-day youth baseball coaches are uncaring. They care deeply, not just about baseball, but about the children themselves. Our argument is that they just have the wrong idea of what's best for children.

Consider the perspective of the children themselves. In a classic study comparing children's and adults' values, Seefeldt, Ewing, and Walk (1992) found that children's top seven values on their list of reasons why they play sports included having fun, improving skills, and experiencing the excitement of competition. The top seven did not include winning. So, if winning is the primary aim in coaching youth baseball, we ask, "Who are the games really for — those coaching or those being coached?"

However, the main reason we are opposed to the ethic that puts winning at the top of the list of values is that behind this approach there is often the wrong idea that children need to be introduced, early on, to an ethic that says only the fittest should survive. According to this way of thinking, children need to be taught what life in the "real world" is all about.

Unfortunately, this "real world" approach to raising children more often turns children off to the real world than it turns children on to competing later on. Many children begin to see this world as "no fun" or not a world worth participating in. Children need years of their own world, years of cultivating the sense that they can make a difference, before they are ready to make a difference in the adult world. All the evidence points to the value of extending childhood, not cutting it short. And that is what we are doing now in the way we have organized youth baseball and youth sports — cut short the childhood days when baseball was a game played by children, for children, and with children in control of the games. Those childhood days need not be over if we can learn how to play "small ball"; that is, if we can learn to be content with the singles and scratch hits that are the occasional moments of glory that any child can experience and that fuel a child's love for baseball. In youth baseball, no one needs to be a star.

All this has led more than a few thoughtful adults to ask, "If backyard sports are so good for children and if organized youth sports today have problems, why not shift the focus away from organized youth sports and back to providing children support to play backyard sports on their own?"

The answers to this question are several, but they all lead to the same conclusion; namely, "We can't," or at least most families today can't ignore organized youth sports and opt instead for promoting backyard sports. Today, dramatic decreases in and access to outdoor play spaces, mothers being unavailable to children playing outdoors because mothers are at work, and neighborhoods being unsafe or at least perceived to be unsafe help explain why there has been a significant decrease in backyard sports (Rivkin, 1995). Add to the mix the fact that today there are many more incentives for children to play indoors, the most obvious being electronic play, and you see why organized youth sports have become so central and backyard sports so secondary. Given this description of the play environment for children growing up in America today, the main question now is not how can we promote backyard sports, but how can we improve organized youth sports so that they fill the vacuum left by the decline in backyard sports where children developed a love for the game?

Our putting love for the game at the heart of coaching youth baseball also comes from our observation that loving baseball (or any sport, for that matter) is a way for children to *thrive*. Unlike having fun, thriving is not just for the moment, something that happens during a practice session or a game and then is over. Thriving runs deep and can last for a very long time. Furthermore, thriving is how we describe anyone who is energized, passionate, and engaged with life. Good things happen when someone thrives.

There is another reason why we suggest you adopt as your main goal that of helping children develop a love for the game. We have observed that children want to improve as players not so much to please their parents, peers or coach, but to please themselves. Therefore, we see your helping children develop as players as a way of meeting their needs and developing a love for the game.

Finally, when your goal is to teach so children develop a love for baseball, then the way you teach is apt to provide a much more positive experience for children than if your main goal is skill development, winning, or even having fun. Having children develop a love for the game as your main goal will help you become much more patient and sensible while teaching in ways that motivate children to play well. Yelling, showing frustration, sitting bad players down for long periods of time, putting kids at risk for injury, drafting teams without considering friendships, or simply making the whole business of acquiring baseball skills a business rather than a game, these and other common practices will no longer have any rational function or place in your coaching approach when your main goal is to help players develop a love for the game. Furthermore, when you coach children so they develop a love for the game, you are more likely to do a better job teaching skills because your entire emphasis will be on supporting players and encouraging their development rather than on winning games.

In sum, this book's main focus throughout is on helping you *teach children how to play baseball so that in the course of their maturing as players, they develop a love for the game.*

Developing the Mind of an Athlete

How do you teach children baseball so that they mature as players and develop a love for the game? Most books and films on teaching children baseball begin with baseball mechanics and drills, often with the appearance that through repetitious drills alone children will develop as players. However, children are not robots. They have minds needing to learn how to make quick decisions about what to do with their bodies as well as how to manage their feelings, all for the purpose of playing good baseball. We begin with talk about the mind of an athlete.

What distinguishes the mind of an athlete is a peculiar ability to react quickly, seemingly without thinking, and an ability to remain focused, calm, and self-motivated, particularly under pressure. With respect to reacting quickly and seemingly without thinking, the developmental sequence is as follows:

Before Instruction	*Instruction and Practice*	*During Games*
Action w/o Thinking	Action with Thinking	Action (seemingly) w/o Thinking

This sequence indicates that on the surface, the accomplished player seems to act like the untutored beginner — impulsive and unreflective. However, the difference between the accomplished player and the beginner is huge. The difference is that the accomplished player has practiced so hard and so well that he or she no longer has to think much while reacting to a baseball or game situation. With the accom-

For children, playing baseball should be about having a very good time (photograph by Jay Reichheld).

plished player, proper mechanics and making good judgments in the field have become committed to what is often referred to as "muscle memory." Actually, what muscle memory refers to are the mind's motor programs that have developed in practice and act so efficiently as to make playing baseball seem mindless.

Our goal is to help children practice good baseball until they develop proper mechanics to the point of their committing good mechanics to muscle memory. During games, we need to let them play the way they have practiced and with little in-game instruction. This is hard for many beginning coaches, and, unfortunately, hard for parents, as well. We will have more to say about the problems of in-game instruction in a later chapter on managing games.

EXPLAINING SO CHILDREN UNDERSTAND

Teaching baseball skills so that children commit good mechanics and judgments in the field to muscle memory requires more than providing precise explanations. It also requires explaining so that children understand what they are being taught. This is the hard part, so it is not surprising that few books or films on teaching baseball to children explain this part in depth. Throughout this book, we will explain what it means to teach baseball so that children understand. To give an idea of what we mean, consider the following two explanations of how to grip a baseball bat. The first way comes from John Monteleone's (2004) popular book on coaching hitting: "Wrap your fingers around the bat, aligning the middle knuckles of the top hand between the second and third set of knuckles of the bottom hand" (p. 2).

This isn't a bad explanation, but for many of us with little spatial intelligence, it is hard to follow and even harder to remember. Compare Monteleone's explanation to the following: "Wrap your fingers around the bat. Now line up the door knocking knuckles. Now turn the top hand slightly to the left (for righties) or right (for lefties) so that the door knocking knuckles don't line up with other knuckles."

Both explanations achieve the correct grip. However, there are important differences, and the differences matter. Furthermore, the differences illustrate principles that will help you explain baseball so that children understand.

We offer four principles to help you explain so children understand. The first principle is suggested in the way Monteleone's explanation requires that we think about more than one relationship at a time. He asks us to think about the various knuckles in relationship to one another—first and second, second and third, first and third. This is hard for adults and impossible for most children to comprehend. From this observation, we derive our first principle of explaining baseball so that children understand: *Avoid explanations that require children to think about more than one relationship at a time.* We'll come back to this principle many times when discussing ways to teach baseball mechanics, so if it isn't clear now, don't worry. It will become clear later on.

What about the second explanation? Does it follow this principle or violate it? With the second explanation, the three-step process means we need to think about only one relationship at a time. First, we are asked to wrap our fingers. Second, we are asked to line up the door knocking knuckles. While there are several fingers and several door knocking knuckles, treating them all the same means we need only to concentrate on wrapping and lining them up—not too difficult even for a child. Third, we are asked to turn the top hand to the left or right; again, not too difficult for a child because there is only one relationship to consider.

Another reason why we prefer the second explanation is that it uses the mental image of knuckles knocking on a door. Mental images help children (and most adults) understand and remember. From this observation we derive the second principle of explaining baseball so children understand: *Use mental images when explaining complex acts such as hitting a baseball.* This principle also will become clear as we move through the book.

There is a third principle not illustrated in the example of explaining how to grip a baseball bat, because gripping a bat is a component of the complex act of hitting. The third principle is: *Break complex skills such as hitting into component skills, and have players practice component skills separately as well as together.* To continue with the example of teaching hitting, this means setting aside time to have players practice gripping a bat properly as well as practice going through the entire process of setting up to hit (gripping bat, assuming proper location in batting box, checking plate coverage, assuming a proper stance).

Therefore, teaching baseball is never a matter of simply teaching by explaining. Teaching baseball is also a matter of getting children to practice what has been explained; **practice makes permanent** and not necessarily perfect. Furthermore, practice moves knowledge stored as words to knowledge stored as motor programs or "muscle memory." This allows for the split-second reactions needed to play almost any sport, including baseball. Therefore, the fourth principle is: *Get children to practice good mechanics the way they have been explained until they commit them to muscle memory.*

This fourth principle may seem self-evident, but it is not. Consider the example of adopting a proper grip on a bat. How many coaches have you observed who have children practice picking up a bat and gripping it correctly or stopping practice sessions to correct an incorrect grip — not just once or twice but for however long it takes for adopting the proper grip to become automatic? We suspect the answer is "none" or "not many." Later on, we will have more to say about the meaning and importance of practicing good mechanics until good mechanics are committed to muscle memory.

MOTIVATING CHILDREN IN POSITIVE WAYS

These four principles have to do with explaining baseball so that children understand and with practice for the purpose of committing good mechanics to muscle memory. However, children can understand baseball mechanics and still not focus, stay calm, remain confident, and remain motivated to improve and play hard. That is, they can understand but still fail to develop a kind of mental toughness and self-motivation that also characterizes the mind of an athlete. Without accomplishing these things, they won't develop a love for the game.

So what can we do to motivate children to develop these motivational aspects of the mind of an athlete? Watch most Little League games, and you will get one answer. Many if not most Little League coaches try to motivate children using *command instructions*. That is, they utter commands to run hard, swing hard, shake off errors, and even commands to stay calm and have fun.

In moderation, there is nothing wrong with command instructions. Indeed, at the beginning phase of teaching proper mechanics, command instructions are necessary to get players to experience proper mechanics. However, when command instructions are used too often or as the only way to motivate, especially when they lead to relentless shouting, they can irritate players, cause undue pressure that undermines players' ability to stay loose, and even frighten players. In short, when over-used or used as the only way to motivate children, command instructions can actually prevent children from developing mental toughness, confidence, and the right frame of mind for playing good baseball. Furthermore, because the method can prevent children from having fun, the instructions can prevent children from developing a love for the game. What children really need from us are positive ways to motivate them and ways that give them more control.

In later chapters, we will have more to say about how you can motivate players through the positive ways you communicate, encourage, teach skills, use a games approach to practices, and give children control by helping them set goals, figure out how to respond to errors, manage anxiety, and learn to read and respond to game situations on their own. Mostly, though, we will try to convince you that the single most important way you can motivate children is to be a coach who cares more for his players than about winning games.

In sum, this book is meant to help you explain baseball so children understand and motivate players in positive ways, all for the purpose of helping children mature as players and develop a love for the game. These two themes of explaining and motivating run throughout the book — as we go from discussing teaching baseball mechanics, to discussing managing practices and games, to discussing building a team culture. However, depending on what is being discussed, only one theme at a time is apt to be emphasized. We turn now to the section on teaching baseball mechanics, where the emphasis is on explaining so children understand.

Part One

Teaching Baseball Mechanics

The main point here is that you can't teach baseball until you know what exactly needs to be taught. What needs to be taught is *baseball mechanics*. Baseball mechanics refers to the correct ways to hit, run the base paths, field, and pitch. We say "correct ways" because, among baseball professionals, there is a great deal of consensus about how to play baseball. For example, everyone agrees that infielders should attack the baseball, hitters should keep their stride foot "quiet," and pitchers should keep both elbows high during the delivery. Therefore, what is explained in this section is not opinion or interpretation but rather the facts about how to play baseball.

Baseball mechanics are complex, so complex that it is easy to overwhelm children or explain mechanics in ways that children cannot possibly understand. In this section, we offer several ways to teach mechanics that are specifically designed for children.

First, we help you teach children by explaining *component skills*. Component skills are those skills that children can experience as wholes without parts. For example, the "stride" is a component skill when hitting, and the "drop step" is a component skill when pitching. Once a component skill is explained and demonstrated, children often can just "do it."

Second, we help you teach component skills by providing you with compelling *mental images* and short phrases that help children visualize what needs to be done, such as saying "Touch the wall" to help children get the idea of how to bring the ball back before throwing.

Third, with younger players, we sometimes suggest substituting a simplified variant of a component skill or eliminating a component skill, such as the "lift" when pitching. We do so whenever we are confident that simplifying or eliminating won't lead to bad habits and will leave a strong foundation to build on.

In this section, each chapter discusses a different complex skill. However, we emphasize throughout your needing to help children *focus attention, adopt a confident-aggressive attitude, and remain balanced while playing.* At the most general level, we suggest you continually teach your players how to focus, adopt a confident-aggressive attitude, and remain balanced.

In this section, we also make clear that *practice makes permanent* and not necessarily perfect. We stress this to be clear about the meaning of practice and how practicing bad mechanics can lead to playing poor baseball.

One other general comment about teaching baseball mechanics to children is that it is natural for anyone, children included, to at first feel scared of getting hurt by a baseball. We suggest using balls softer than baseballs, for example, tennis balls or, better yet, "rag" balls, while teaching and practicing baseball mechanics. Once children develop reasonably good mechanics, you can use real baseballs to continue with their training. If obtaining softer balls is impractical, then at least avoid forcing young players to field hard-hit ground balls and line drives.

As you read through this section, try to do more than understand what we are explaining and suggesting. Try also to visualize what we are explaining and suggesting, and then try to hit, field, and pitch using what you have just read. Doing so will put you in a better position to understand the experience of your players when you try to teach them. Your being able to coach children will depend on your adopting a double focus—one focus being on images in your head of how to play the game correctly, and another focus being on what your players are experiencing and doing in response to your instructions. Therefore, your trying to coach yourself using what you have read in this section on mechanics should help you be able to adopt this double focus.

1

Offense: Hitting, Bunting and Baserunning

Hitting a baseball properly requires adopting a proper grip, stance, stride, load, hip rotation, weight distribution, swing, and follow through — all the while keeping the head steady and both eyes riveted on the ball. As this description indicates, hitting is complex, meaning it is no easy task to explain hitting to children.

In this chapter, we will explain hitting and give you the knowledge and strategies you will need for teaching each and every player. Some of your players may be able to master only a few of the basics, such as proper grip, stance, and swinging down and through the ball. This is important to keep in mind, because one of your main challenges will be to determine which aspects of hitting a player is ready, willing, and able to learn. However, many and perhaps most of your players will be able to use everything you have to give them, so understanding the mechanics of hitting will help you coach them more effectively.

We suggest that you take what we explain and try it yourself with a batting tee or some other way to practice hitting. Doing so will ensure that you have the knowledge needed to teach players how to hit. Furthermore, you will learn for yourself that certain aspects of hitting are harder to master than others; that's good to know when you are teaching children.

Setting Up to Hit

Before actually hitting, players need to learn how to choose the right bat, adopt the correct grip, and assume a proper stance. Since these do not depend on athletic ability, every player should be able to learn them.

CHOOSING THE RIGHT BAT

A bat should be heavy enough to feel powerful but light enough to generate bat speed. The challenge is to find a bat with the right *weight*. This is especially important for young players who on their own often select excessively heavy bats that lead to bad hitting habits.

A good test to determine proper weight is to have players hold a bat with their glove hand straight out, to the side, and with their arm fully extended. Then have them spell their name with the bat, keeping the elbow locked and the arm above shoulder height. If the arm starts to shake, the bat is too heavy. This test can be used until maximum weight is supported without shaking.

With the advent of aluminum bats, leagues for adolescents are apt to have a "minus three" rule. The rule was installed to protect pitchers from the faster line drives that can occur when using aluminum bats. This rule limits the choice of bat to those whose weight minus their length results in minus three or less. For example, a bat 31 inches in length can weigh no more than 28 ounces.

GRIP

Check to see that players hold the bat at the intersection of their fingers and palms, not across the middle of their palms.

The grip should be firm but not so firm as to restrict movement of the wrists and forearms. Check to see that your players don't squeeze the bat tightly, but rather keep their grip loose until actually going into the load and swing. As a pre-swing

Testing for correct bat weight.

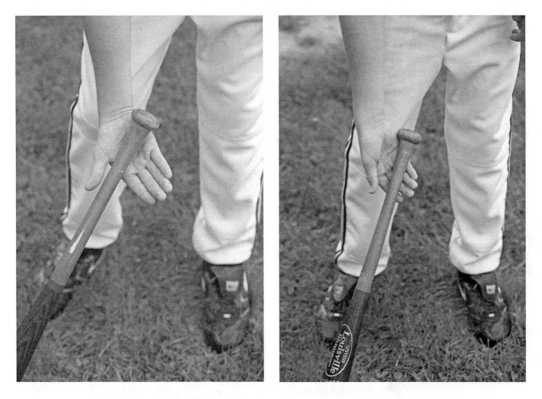

Incorrect palm grip.   Correct finger grip.

movement designed to relax the fingers, encourage those who have trouble relaxing to "milk" the bat.

As suggested in the introduction, tell players to wrap their fingers around the bat. Then tell them to line up the door knocking knuckles. Then tell them to turn the top hand slightly to the left (for righties) or to the right (for lefties) so that the door knocking knuckles don't line up with other knuckles.

This grip will seem odd and uncomfortable at first since younger players naturally use a "motorcycle" grip with the knuckles of each hand aligned. However, even though it may feel odd and uncomfortable, with practice the proper grip will become habit. It is the best grip because it provides the swing with an extra "whip" and ensures that when the bat hits the ball, the hands will be positioned to provide maximum force.

PLATE COVERAGE AND LOCATION OF FEET

For proper plate coverage, the bat should reach the outside corner of the plate. A good test for this is to have a player grasp the bat handle while leaning slightly forward and resting the end of the bat on the outside corner of the plate. The player should feel comfortable doing so.

As for the location of the feet, we recommend that younger players start with their front foot lined up to the middle of the plate. This will place them somewhat back in the box, giving them a slightly longer time to see the ball before hitting.

Testing for plate coverage.

Lining up front foot.

STANCE

We recommend an *even* stance where players have their feet line up so that a bat laying on the ground and resting in front of and against each foot will point directly at the pitcher. However, what is most important is getting your players into a *balanced* stance by having them assume the *athlete's position*. In the athlete's position, the feet are slightly more than shoulder-width apart. The knees are bent. The back is slightly bent over, and the head is turned so that both eyes face the pitcher.

In a proper stance, the front arm should be stretched back across the chest so that the hands are positioned approximately 1–2 inches in front of the back shoulder. Furthermore, the hands should be "cocked"—that is, slightly turned up at the wrists to create a whipping action. Younger players need not attend to this detail.

The bat should be over the back shoulder at about a 45-degree angle, not straight up, laying down or wrapped around the neck. Having the bat at a 45-degree angle allows for the most efficient path to the ball and prevents problems such as uppercutting.

Poor Balance

Many young players have poor balance from the start because they stand too upright, with their feet not far enough apart. Some have poor balance because they dance or shuffle their feet as the ball is being thrown. A player's batting won't improve until good balance is developed.

* * *

You can help a player establish balance by repeatedly demonstrating proper balance and having the player model the balanced stance before every hit at practice. Players can also practice balance by jumping off the ground in the athlete's position and resuming the stance upon landing.

A Misguided Tip

Perhaps the most frequent misguided tip is "Keep the back elbow up!" In fact, keeping the back elbow too high will cause players to take a slow, rounded path to the baseball. Instead, the back elbow should remain in a comfortable position, not too high and not too low.

The Stride and Load

Together, the stride and load are pre-swing movements that help players get ready to swing with precision and power. The stride is for timing and balance. The load is for precision and power. This is one of the hardest parts of hitting for beginning players to learn: how to stride properly while "loading up" before, not during, the swing and how to do so slowly and under control. Check constantly to see that players are both striding and loading slowly. The stride and load begin during the pitcher's windup and before the ball is actually released.

THE STRIDE

The stride, or side step, directly toward the pitcher with the front foot should be short, closed, and light (or "quiet," as some prefer to say). Depending on a player's height, the stride can range anywhere from 3–6 inches. During the stride, the weight should remain *back* and not on the front foot. Often, younger players over-stride

Incorrect upright stance.

Correct stance.

Incorrect bat angle — too straight up.

Incorrect bat position — wrapped around neck.

Correct 45-degree bat angle.

Preventing over-striding.

or lunge, resulting in their shifting their weight too soon and over the front foot, or they begin their swing as they stride. Both mistakes diminish power by eliminating the action of the lower body, especially the hips. Watch for these mistakes, and if they happen, correct them immediately. One way to correct for over-striding is to place a bat several inches from and parallel to the stride (front) foot (see bottom photograph on this page).

To help players keep their weight back during the stride, have them imagine themselves stepping out onto a pond covered by thin ice. They should be stepping out so as to not fall in. Doing so will help players keep most of their weight on the back leg, where it belongs. Another method for keeping their weight back is to eliminate the stride altogether and replace it by simply raising up the front foot or raising only the heel of the front foot — enough to ensure that weight stays back.

Younger players are also apt to open up their front foot as they stride, or bring it back (in other words, "step in the bucket"). Teach them to instead keep the stride foot closed or only slightly open; that is, only slightly turned toward the pitcher. To correct for stepping in the bucket, place a bat directly behind the batter's feet.

THE LOAD

The load refers to moving the hands back and up, or "cocking," before beginning the actual swing, as well as to

---

Ways to Correct Problems with the Stride

Many young players have a tendency to stride too far, lunge, open up their stride, "step in the bucket," or begin their swing as they stride. Lunging and over-striding happen when a player steps too far and too heavy during the stride phase of hitting. When lunging or over-striding, players will often bring their weight directly over the lead foot, which results in a loss of power. You can correct these mistakes by repeatedly demonstrating a correct stride—and by having a player practice striding properly.

"Stepping in the bucket" refers to the front foot stepping away from the plate, which indicates a player is afraid of getting hit by the ball. One remedy is to have players hit while their feet are in separate automobile tires or while a baseball bat is lying on the ground and directly behind both legs.

If the stride proves too difficult for some players, eliminate the stride altogether. Instead, have them keep their weight on their back leg and then have them pick up the heel of their front foot while transferring their weight forward without actually moving the foot forward.

---

moving the body so as to create torque. When hitting, you have to move back before you move forward. Doing so should stretch the lead arm so that it ends up close to the body. The load and stride begin simultaneously.

During the load phase, the hands move up and back in front of the back shoulder (not further), where they should stop just long enough to allow them to explode down and through the baseball. If the hands do not go back far enough or go back too far, players will have limited power as well as trouble hitting balls on the outside corner of the plate. If the hands are too low or too high before the swing, players will swing with an uppercut.

To create torque or coil in the body, we also recommend having players rotate their front hip slightly and bend their inside knee slightly inward. This is a fine point that can be overlooked without much loss.

The Swing

A proper swing involves the whole body and careful use of the eyes, head, shoulders, hips, feet, and hands. The swing uses the body to "punch" the bat directly down and through the ball and then have a significant follow-through.

Using the Body as a Rubber Band

Have players "load up" by imagining they are a rubber band drawing back. To reinforce this image and to demonstrate that proper load increases not only power but also precision, draw a rubber band only partway back and launch it at a specific target. Next draw the rubber band all the way back and launch it at the same target. The second try should produce not only more power, but also better precision. Keeping with the rubber band image, have players really stretch their lead arm across their chest and turn their front knee slightly inward in this pre-swing phase of hitting.

To better remember what it means to punch and follow-through, use the saying, *"Short to it, and long through it."*

Get players to envision hitting line drives up the middle. Doing so will help them correct a natural tendency to open up their stance too soon and try to pull the ball. Their opening up too soon and trying to pull the ball leads to their head moving, which in turn leads to missing the ball.

EYES AND HEAD

A proper swing depends on players closely watching the ball all the way onto the bat. It is not enough for you, as a coach, to say, "Watch the ball." As a coach, you must teach your players how to watch the ball.

First, players must watch the baseball with both eyes — from the instant the ball becomes visible in the pitcher's windup until the ball hits the sweet spot of the bat in front of the plate. Players should maintain a *soft focus* on the pitcher until the moment the pitcher releases the ball. At the release point, players should adopt a *hard focus*, one that rivets the eyes on the ball all the way from the pitcher's hand to when it hits the bat.

Players can be helped to watch the ball all the way onto the bat by having them attempt to see the seams of the ball and by having them pretend they are radar-tracking devices "locking onto" an enemy missile. Since players tend to look up during the swing (especially just before the ball arrives), constantly impress upon them to watch the ball onto the bat.

SHOULDERS

Before the swing, the inside shoulder (the shoulder closest to the pitcher) should stay closed, that is, not face the pitcher. Opening up too soon takes the

Front shoulder opens up too soon.   **Front shoulder stays closed.**

eyes off the ball and dips the back shoulder, making it difficult to maintain focus and balance. The inside shoulder should begin to open up only as the hands move down to the point of contact.

BACK KNEE AND HIP

After providing a slight pre-swing coil with their upper body and possibly with their front knee turned inward, players should *drive their back knee and hip* through the swing so that the belt buckle ends up facing the pitcher and the *front leg ends up straight,* not bent. Driving the back knee and hip through the swing while the front leg is straight provides bat speed and therefore power. Tell your players to think of the back knee as the *trigger* that sets the swing into motion.

26

HANDS

Right before the swing, players must move their hands back and up slightly, with the wrists cocked or bent slightly upward, waiting until *the last possible instant* before exploding down and through the hitting zone. Once the back knee has triggered the start of the swing, the hands move the knob of the bat down and for a moment, directly pointed at the baseball. The hands move straight *down and through* the hitting zone while remaining close to the body — not extended out over the plate. Extending the hands and arms away from the body is a common problem for beginners; correct it as soon as you see it. During the swing, if players fail to keep their hands and arms in toward the body, they will hit weakly with their arms and upper body only.

Dropping the Hands

Young players sometimes drop their hands just before or while swinging. As a result, they resort to a roundhouse swing. Help for this mistake can come from repeated demonstrations of how to keep the hands going straight down and through the baseball and by having players put down their bat and practice "slapping" down and through.

At the moment the bat hits the ball, the palm of the hitter's top hand (usually the throwing hand) should be under the bat handle and facing up, while the palm of the other hand should be above the bat handle and facing down. This is possible if the batter has assumed a proper grip. At this moment, the bat should be level (parallel) to the ground. Once in this position, the hands and wrists explode the barrel of the bat through the hitting zone and then naturally "roll over" to allow for a proper follow through. Check carefully to see that young players do not roll their hands over too early in the swing but rather wait for that moment when the bat is level to the ground.

The top picture on the following page illustrates everything said here about *the positioning of the hips, hands, and front leg at the moment of contact.*

FOLLOW THROUGH

As already mentioned, when hitting, most young players try to pull the ball. In doing so, they often miss the ball altogether. Therefore, teach your players to swing through the baseball as if they are trying to hit two baseballs, with an imag-

Moment of contact.

The follow through.

inary one coming immediately after the first real baseball. They should be trying to punch the baseball(s) directly back toward the pitcher. Teaching your players to punch the ball back toward the pitcher will create more contact as well as more line drives, which are essential to successful hitting.

Also stress the need to follow all the way through, even on misses. This is especially important for younger players, because many younger players stop their follow through prematurely. At the end of the follow through, the hands should finish somewhere close to the front shoulder, neither too far above nor too far below.

If the hands end up finishing too far above the shoulder, it usually indicates an uppercut swing. If the hands finish too far below the shoulder, it usually means the top hand is not rolling over during contact with the ball or the arms are not extending properly through the point of contact. And if there is no follow through, it means players probably haven't kept their weight back. The follow through and finish should be the same every time.

Bunting

Bunting is hitting without swinging the bat. Learning to bunt the right way requires several considerations, including *watching the ball into the hitting zone or until the point of contact* all the while *maintaining a "quiet" body.* The end goal for a bunter is to place the ball on the ground 10–20 feet to the outside, not in front of home plate.

When *bunting for a hit*, the batter tries to catch the defense off-guard by waiting until the last second and then angling the ball down the first or third base line. The bunt for a hit, or drag bunt (because left-handed bunters often "drag" the ball down the first base line), requires the batter to get out of the box as quickly as possible. Ideally, the batter adopts a pivot stance when bunting for a base hit, but for younger players the regular, open stance is likely to be more reliable.

THE HANDS

Proper bunting mechanics requires the bottom hand (left hand for righties, right hand for lefties) to remain stationary at the handle end of the bat, with the top hand shifting halfway up the bat. The top hand's thumb should be on the top of the bat while the other fingers are positioned on the bottom of the bat.

Pinching the bat.

Tell players to "pinch" instead of hold the bat and in such a way that the ball won't hit their fingers.

Before contact, the bat should be out in front of the hitter and held upward at a 45-degree angle. Maintaining an angled bat prior to contact gives the batter the control and flexibility needed to adjust to a wide variety of pitches. An excessively angled bat will make it harder for the ball to be bunted, and an insignificantly angled bat will result in a pop-up. At the point of contact, the bat should be angled so that it is parallel to the ground.

THE FEET

Bunters must be in a position to see the entire ball. Thus, they must turn their hips slightly toward the pitcher, or pivot. The pivot stance requires the back foot and back knee to turn (similar to a hitter's "squish the bug" technique) while the front foot remains closed. In this pivot stance, the batter's chest will be facing toward the pitcher, with hips slightly open. Bunting with the chest facing the

The pivot stance for bunting.

Bat level for bunting.

pitcher is advantageous because the bunter has a clear view of the ball throughout its path, making it easier for the batter to bring his bat back to take a bad pitch or to change his mind and bring the bat back to swing on a good pitch.

Some coaches prefer to have batters square the hips to the pitcher and to bring both feet up toward the plate. This method, which is easier to execute (a good method for younger players), forces hitters to see the ball for as long as possible.

THE LEGS

While bunting, the lower body should be in the athlete's position: legs spread and knees bent slightly so the body's weight is on the balls of the feet. On pitches that are high or low, the bat's angle should not change. Instead, the batter's knees should be lower on low pitches and higher on high pitches. While the pitch is approaching the plate, batters should prevent all movement in the hips and legs. A "*quiet*" or motionless body will help the batter see the ball all the way into the hitting zone.

Once the ball is ready to be bunted, the angle of the bat will change. The bat will move from a 45-degree position into a flatter position at the point of contact. It is a natural action to flatten a bat's angle when executing a bunt.

Upon contact, the bat should *absorb* the baseball so that the ball is

30

The sacrifice bunt.

not bunted too far. Tell players to think of the bat as a fielder's glove absorbing the ball into the glove. The bunter should gently absorb the ball onto the bat so that it stops 10–20 feet away from the plate.

The *sacrifice bunt* is when the batter's only job is to advance a runner to the next base. A sacrifice bunt should only be executed when the pitcher throws a strike. The batter should square around to bunt when the pitcher's hand goes back to throw. With a runner on first, the ball should be bunted in the grassy area between the pitcher's mound and first base. Bunting down the first base line requires the batter to extend his bottom hand toward the first base bag so that the bat's angle is directed toward the base.

With a runner on second, the ball should be bunted between the pitcher's mound and third base in order to force the third baseman to leave the base open. To do this, the batter must bring his bottom hand in toward his body. The knob of the bat should be moving closer to the stomach, and the bat's angle should be directed down the third base bag.

The *squeeze bunt* is a bunt when the batter's goal is to score the runner from third. In a "suicide squeeze," the runner will be sprinting home as the batter is bunting the ball. (This tactic is against the rules for younger children in Little League.) The batter should bunt any ball that is pitched or else the runner will be tagged out. The batter should assume a bunting position only after the pitcher releases the ball, so as to not give away too soon that he is bunting. For this play to work, the batter need not produce a perfect bunt. He needs only to put the ball on the ground!

FAKING THE BUNT

There will be times during most games when faking a bunt helps to draw a walk or helps a runner trying to steal a base. Therefore, teach your players how to fake a bunt by having them practice executing a pivot stance and drawing the bat back at the last moment before a pitch crosses the plate.

Teaching Players How to Avoid Being Hit

One more important matter when teaching younger players how to hit involves putting aside time to teach them how to avoid being hit. Many beginning players will do the wrong thing when a pitcher throws at them. Rather than duck back and out of the way, they will duck directly into the path of the ball — scary to watch and even scarier when a ball hits their head. Therefore, spend whatever time it takes to teach players to spin down and away from the pitch, thus protecting their heads.

The wrong way to avoid being hit.   The correct way to avoid being hit.

Baserunning

Baserunning may appear to be something that need not be taught. After all, children know how to run. However, in baseball there are rules about baserunning, rules that may seem obvious to you, but that young players may not know. Here is one humorous example (except for the coach's reaction) of what we mean.

When the Rules of Baserunning Aren't Self-Evident

In one Little League game, Eric, age 10, had gotten on base and made it to second. At some point, the catcher overthrew the pitcher, and the ball rolled to a stop about three feet from the base. Eric promptly went over to the ball, picked it up, and handed it to the second baseman—at which point, the umpire called him out.

As he made his way to the bench, his coach approached him and said, "What were you thinking?" Eric looked confused, lowered his eyes, sat down on the bench, and for the rest of the inning appeared to have no enthusiasm for the game in progress.

Like every other aspect of playing baseball, young players need coaching to understand the rules of baserunning. Most of all, they need coaching in the proper ways to run the bases. This means they need to be taught how to run through first base, turn corners, get off bases quickly, read situations so as to use good judgment, follow the base coaches' directions, and slide properly.

Begin by teaching players how to get out of the batter's box. The key here is to get them to lean toward first base, take quick short steps, and pump their arms. These three actions will get players out of the box and headed to first as quickly as they can.

Running from Home to First

On balls hit to the infield, teach your players to *sprint to and through* first base. When running, eyes must be on first base, not on the ball in play. When reaching first base, players should hit the front part of the base and run through the base without slowing down and then look immediately over their right shoulder to see if there is an overthrow. Once players run through the base, they should avoid entering the field of play, which could make them liable to being tagged out. With younger players, it will be enough to simply get them to run through first base. If there is an overthrow, runners should stop and then take a 90-degree turn and head to second base, with no roundhouse path needed or desired.

On balls hit to the outfield, players should sprint to first base *thinking second*, that is, thinking they will be going to second base. Before reaching first base, they should take a *banana path* towards the base in order to touch the inside part of the bag and be positioned to run straight to second. A banana path is not the same as a last-second rounding off; a banana path has players rounding into the bag and toward second without slowing down.

After rounding first base, players should immediately find the ball in the outfield, and then either wait for audible instructions from a coach or, if it is clear they can make it safely to second, sprint to second base. Even if it seems a fly ball will be caught or a line drive to the outfield will be fielded cleanly, players should round first and go at least one-third to half way to second — both to be ready should an error occur and to force outfielders to hurry their throw. This kind of aggressive baserunning needs to be practiced because young ballplayers do not naturally know how to be aggressive on the base paths.

Running through first base.

On the Bases

If the rule is no leadoffs, have players anticipate the ball crossing the plate and push or "pop" off with their dominant foot, taking two steps regardless of whether the ball is hit or not. During practice sessions, have players practice "popping" of the bag.

If the rule allows for leads, when leading off first base, players should shuffle off the bag and assume the ready position (not be flat footed), directly face the pitcher, and if the pitcher throws over, dive back into the bag while keeping the body low. When leading off the bag, players should have their eyes focused on the baseball and where it goes when it leaves the bat.

On grounders, players should sprint; on short pop-ups and line drives, they should hold up; and on fly balls they should leave the base and hold up about half way between first and second, watching the ball and awaiting instructions from coaches.

A player practicing running through first base and checking to see if there is an overthrow (photograph by Jay Reichheld).

RUNNING FROM SECOND TO HOME

On a ball hit to the outfield, players will take a path similar to going from home to second. However, when going from second to home, because the ball will be out of the player's sight, the player depends entirely on the third base coach for instructions. Players should leave second base paying close attention to the third base coach. If they are given the green light (waved home), they should hit the inside corner of the base and sprint to home. Teach players to watch the third base coach and respond to his instructions.

RUNNING FROM THIRD TO HOME AND TAGGING UP

Here, players are dependent on auditory instruction from the third base coach. With less than two outs, it should be the player's as well as the coach's responsibility to read the ball off the bat. If the ball is hit downwards, the player advances unless the ball is hit directly to the pitcher or to an infielder pulled in. If the ball goes upwards or on a line, the player holds up and waits for auditory instruction from the coach. If there are less than two outs and a long fly ball is hit to the outfield, the player holds the base and, if the coach says to tag up, sprints home once the ball *touches* any part of the outfielder or hits the ground.

Sliding

Sliding feet-first into bases other than first base is obligatory in Little League baseball. Sliding must be taught properly. For most players, the natural way to slide is with the left leg extended and the right leg folded underneath. However, it is permissible to reverse this order.

When running towards a base, players should begin their slide approximately one and a half body lengths away from the bag or base. First, they should already have begun to slow down by dropping their hips towards the ground and by bending their knees slightly. Then they should leave their feet and simply *sit down*, extending their left leg and folding their right leg underneath. Contact with the ground should be made with the upper hamstring of their right leg.

Once contact is made with the ground, players should be sitting fully upright, with both hands in the air to prevent them from scraping on the ground and causing injury. After contact with the ground, momentum will naturally take players forward so as to make contact with the base.

Sliding headfirst or diving into a base is illegal in Little League baseball because doing so could lead to dangerous head, neck, or spinal cord injuries. Sliding head first and diving should be avoided at the youth level.

What to Look for When Hitting

Look for positive signs of:

1. A balanced stance with proper grip and bat angle.
2. A slow, under control stride and load prior to the swing.
3. A swing that moves down and through the ball with hands close to the body, head steady, and eyes looking at the ball.
4. During the swing, weight kept on the back foot and hips rotating to get the back hip to drive the ball.
5. A full follow through that ends at or near the front shoulder.

Taking a banana path.

Look especially for the following problems:

1. Wrong grip (e.g., motorcycle grip).
2. Unbalanced stance (usually upright).
3. Bat angled incorrectly — too high, too low, or wrapped around the neck.
4. Over striding, stepping in the bucket, and failing to keep weight on the back foot.
5. Striding and loading too quickly.
6. Swinging too soon or with hands and arms out over the plate.
7. Upper cutting — roundhouse swing.
8. Failure to punch the ball up the middle by trying to pull the ball.
9. No follow through or a follow through that is too high or too low.

What to Look for When Bunting

1. A balanced stance.
2. Correct pivot and positioning of hands.

Correct slide.

3. Proper bat angle before and during contact with the ball.
4. Absorbing the ball into the bat.

What to Look for When Baserunning

1. Running through first base on ground balls to the infield.
2. Taking a banana path and positioning correctly to judge whether to go to second or stay at first.
3. Listening to instructions from the third base coach when running from second to home or from third to home.
4. If no leads are allowed, "popping" off the bag when the ball crosses the plate.
5. If leads are allowed, taking the lead during the pitcher's wind-up and at a reasonable distance from the bag.

2

Playing the Field: Throwing, Catching and Fielding

Unlike batting and pitching skills, fielding skills are often experienced as relatively simple and straightforward, even though they are not. In fact, teaching fielding skills presents the same kinds of challenges as when teaching hitting and pitching. Furthermore, without good coaching, fielding skills are not likely to develop on their own.

Choosing and Caring for a Glove

Anyone who has spent time watching youth baseball is apt to have seen a child using a glove better suited for a very big man. The visual effect can be comical. Unfortunately, the effect on the child's play is not comical. Too large a glove translates into poor play. So advise your players and their parents to choose a glove that is not too big.

Once that appropriately sized glove is chosen, the other rule is to keep it in good condition, which means training the glove to remain *open*. This may be done by occasionally using small amounts of leather conditioner and, more important, by leaving a ball in the pocket of the glove when it isn't being used.

Share this information not only with your players but also with their parents — both to ensure that players take care of their glove and to instill an attitude and habit of mind about playing baseball. Caring for a glove (or bat) can develop into caring for baseball.

Fielding properly requires learning how *to set* to field a baseball, how *to attack* the ball, how *to receive or catch* the ball, how *to transfer the ball to a throwing position,* and how *to throw* the ball to a specific target. This is true for infielders as

Choose a glove not too big.

well as for outfielders. However, since there are important details distinguishing infield play from outfield play, we will discuss each in turn.

Infield Play

Before every pitch, infielders should adopt a confident-aggressive mindset. Specifically, they should prepare mentally for a sharp ground ball and wish that the batter hits them the ball. You

Leave a ball in the glove's pocket.

can instill this confident-aggressive mindset directly, for example, by yelling out during groundball drills, "Who is ready?" or "Who wants the ball?" and having your players yell out, "I am" and "I want the ball."

Also before every pitch, infielders should adopt a *"ready" or "athlete's" position*. As mentioned in the previous chapter, the athlete's position consists of adopting a slightly wider stance than for standing, leaning over slightly with weight on the balls of the feet and balanced so that the body is ready to move quickly in any direction. Adopting the ready or athlete's position on every play may be too much to ask of younger players (ages eight to ten), so be careful to reinforce those who try and to not be overly demanding on those who do not.

THE SET

The set refers to the movement of a fielder at the start of a pitcher's wind-up. Just before the pitcher winds up to throw, fielders should have one leg back, similar to a pitcher's drop step. At the start of the wind-up, fielders should move this back leg forward and stop at the moment the pitcher releases the ball so that the fielder's weight is on the balls of the feet and the glove is in front of the body. This movement is the *set*.

Alternatively, the set can be a two-step process sometimes referred to as *creeping*. This entails starting with the feet parallel to one another at the beginning of the pitcher's wind-up and followed by two short steps forward and stopping when the pitcher releases the ball. Some players prefer one or the other; it really does not matter. What matters is getting ready to field a ball by moving before the pitch.

Encourage players to adopt whichever set movement feels the most natural. However, whether the set is a one-step or two-step process, the end result should be a player in the "athlete's" position, ready to "pounce" and attack a ground ball.

Fielding Like a Predator

Prior to the pitcher releasing the ball, when creeping or taking their single step forward in a low, crouched position with glove in front of the body, infielders should be thinking of themselves as predators in the jungle, eager to pounce with speed and agility on their prey. As with a wild predator, a fielder's momentum should be moving forward and toward the prey—the soon-to-be-batted ball. Outfielders too should take a predatory step, but because they must cover longer distances and be more concerned about balls hit over their head, they should not be bent over as much or be quite so aggressive in their set.

The set prevents fielders from becoming flat-footed and unable to make a play on a ground ball, particularly one slightly out of reach. Furthermore, the set

The set (creeping).   The end of the set.

reinforces an aggressive attitude, one that we liken to that of a predator. Insisting on the set for younger players may be too much, and so for younger players, the set is something to encourage, not require.

The Attack

The attack refers to the action taken by the fielder immediately after the ball has been hit. It is when the fielder moves towards the batted ball in anticipation of fielding it. On balls hit to an infielder, teach your players to *beat the ball to the spot*. To help with this concept of beating the ball to the spot, have your infielders make an imaginary line in the dirt, several steps in front of them. The line should mark a barrier where no ball is allowed to pass.

Infielders must always work to cut the ball off at an angle. That is, they should avoid sitting back. Sitting back and passively letting the ball come to the fielder allows a runner more time to advance. Also, sitting back causes late throws, and late throws are more likely to be rushed throws, resulting in errors. Finally, sitting back increases the chances of getting a bad hop.

Beating the ball to the spot.

Not getting the glove down.

RECEIVING GROUND BALLS

When attacking ground balls, many young infielders make the mistake of tucking their gloves into their bodies, making it necessary for them to stab at the ball, which increases the likelihood they will miss the ball altogether. What they should do as they attack the ball is *keep their glove in front of them.*

For ground balls hit right at a player, teach your players to move forward and be extra careful to get the glove down. With ground balls hit right at a player, the tendency is to wait longer to get the glove down. Doing so will often result in ground balls going under the glove and into the outfield.

For balls hit not too hard and to the throwing hand side of a player, teach players to take a path to the ball that avoids having to backhand the ball; that is, that keeps the ball in front. Doing so will avoid having to perform the more difficult task of backhanding the ball.

In receiving ground balls, both hands should be out, with the glove hand on the ground and the throwing hand on top to welcome the ball into the glove. The rear end and hat brim should be down. The back should be flat, and the eyes should be watching the ball into the glove. To help them remember, tell players to form a triangle, with the points of the triangle being the feet and the glove.

Receiving with hands out and glove down.

Receiving with rear end and hat brim down.

In receiving the ball into the glove, occasionally the ball will pop out of the glove. However, if the throwing hand is stationed above the glove, the ball will hit that hand and land back securely into the glove. Have your players think of the hand and glove as framing the mouth of an *alligator*, with the glove acting as the alligator's lower jaw and the throwing hand acting as its upper jaw.

We repeat: Infielders must *watch* the ball into the glove, as illustrated in all of the previous examples. Not doing so is a major cause of infield errors. In your coaching, emphasize the importance of receiving balls out in front and watching the ball into the glove.

Hand and glove making alligator mouth.

TRANSFERRING THE BALL TO A THROWING POSITION

Players should also receive ground balls out in front to ensure a quick transfer of the ball from glove to throwing hand. The quick transfer is aided by *absorbing* the ball and glove into the body as the body turns to align itself to the target. As the ball hits the pocket of the glove, players should bring the glove from out in front of the body, inward to the body, and then go immediately to the throwing position.

One of the more subtle features of a good transfer is the special care given to the ball during the transfer. To instill this attitude of caring for the ball, have your players image the ball as something they would normally want to take special care of—a baby, a plate of their favorite food, an egg with a chick inside. The images can vary, and it's fine if the image settled on is silly. Whatever the image, it should be memorable and evoke this attitude of taking care of the ball.

Simplifying the Transfer

For younger players, absorbing the ball while aligning the body to the target can be a difficult skill to perfect. Many younger players have a hard enough time just fielding the ball cleanly. Therefore, with younger players, you can eliminate this component skill of quickly transferring from receiving to throwing. Instead, concentrate on teaching them to simply field the ball cleanly by keeping their glove out in front, their hands positioned properly, their rear end down, and their eyes riveted on the ball.

RECEIVING BALLS THROWN OR HIT IN THE AIR

The key here is keeping the hands together and in front of the chest; no unnecessary one-hand catches to the side. Of course, line drives and errant throws to the side will require receiving balls with one hand. However, teach your players to try always to catch with both hands together and in front of the chest.

THROWING

Throwing a baseball properly requires knowing how to *grip* and *release* the baseball as well as knowing how to use the *eyes*, *arms* and *feet* to create power and accuracy.

Teach your players the "C-grip." The "C-grip" requires placing two fingers

Absorbing the ball during transfer.

Aligning to the target during transfer.

Incorrectly catching to the side.

Correctly catching in front of the chest.

(three for younger players) on top of the baseball and the thumb underneath, leaving a small space between the ball and palm. This grip leads players to throw with their fingertips, which gives greater *velocity*.

The best "C-grip" has the fingers gripping the ball across the four seams at their widest gap. When throwing the ball "over the top" rather than side-arming, gripping the four seams creates the right spin to ensure greater *accuracy*.

Have younger players practice getting the right grip by having them repeatedly throw a ball into their glove and pull it out quickly using the four-seam "C-grip."

As with hitting and pitching, throwing requires fixing the eyes on a target. For infielders this means shifting from watching the ball into the glove to fixing their eyes on a target—almost always on a teammate covering a particular base. Throwing errors often occur because a player has not fixed his eyes on a target.

When throwing, teach your players to keep their lead elbow up to about shoulder height and pointed directly at the target. A player should use this elbow as a guide or way to "*sight the target.*" You can, in fact, use this language to teach players how to position the lead arm elbow by telling them to look down the lead arm to "sight the target." Even while your players are in the midst of practicing fielding ground balls, you can remind them to "Sight the target!"—though not in so commanding a way as to create the kind of stress that can be counter–productive.

At the same time the lead arm goes up and out, the throwing arm reaches back to *touch an imaginary wall*. The elbow of the throwing arm should be raised to shoulder height and bent to about 90 degrees. The forearm and hand should be pointing back and up. However, you don't have to explain all these details if a player understands what is meant when you say "Touch the wall." This is the beauty of using a mental image to explain; it captures the whole without having to explain the parts. In short, just before throwing or delivering a baseball, players should be sighting a target while their throwing arm reaches back to touch an imaginary wall.

Before the delivery phase of the

Four-seam "C-grip."

Touching the wall.

Stepping to the target.

throw and given enough time, the player takes a shuffle step toward the target before pulling the arm back to throw. Doing so brings the lower body into the throw — important for both accuracy and power.

During the delivery, the front shoulder remains closed to the target until the ball is released. The same is true for the hips. That is, the front shoulder and hips should remain closed until the ball is released. Also during the delivery, the front foot should be open and pointed directly at the target. Since so many younger players fail to point their front foot directly at the target, remind them often to "Step to the target" — again, in a way that encourages rather than commands.

The stride, or step forward, should be short so that the player keeps his balance. The back foot should be perpendicular to the target so that the player can push off the back foot and get momentum going toward the target.

For accuracy, players should release the ball over the top rather than throw side-arm. During the release, the glove should be brought to the chest, and the glove arm's elbow should come down rapidly to the side — both to get the glove arm out of the way and to provide extra power through the turning force, called "torque."

After the release, the player's lead arm should naturally fall down to the glove side, and the player's chest should end up over his front knee. In this way, a player's weight will properly shift forward and toward the target after the throw. If the player throws without transferring his weight forward, the throw will not have enough velocity. Check closely for whether players end up with their chest over their front knee.

Outfield Play

Almost everything that has been said about infield play applies to outfield play as well, including the set, the attack, receiving and throwing. However, outfielders must be first and foremost ready to go after and catch fly balls. Furthermore, outfielders must take as their primary responsibility that of preventing balls from getting past them.

GOING AFTER FLY BALLS

As with infielders, outfielders must beat the ball to the spot, especially on balls hit in the air. Therefore, teach your outfielders to read the fly ball quickly and *sprint* to where the ball is anticipated to come down, all the while keeping their *eyes fixed on the ball*. Doing so will make it easier for an outfielder to track the ball, change directions if necessary, and be ready to call off other fielders.

Locking in on Fly Balls

One useful metaphor for explaining how outfielders should sprint to a fly ball is to tell them to *lock in on the ball*, as if they are radar devices locking in on a missile or enemy airplane. During practice and when hitting fly balls, you can reinforce this idea by continually calling out, "Lock in! Lock in!"

We can't over-stress your needing to teach your outfielders to read quickly, sprint to the ball and keep their eyes fixed on the ball — because without coaching, young players tend to react slowly, drift to the ball, and lose track of the ball altogether. The result is dropped balls or playable balls dropping in front of or behind the outfielders. Getting a quick read and jump on fly balls takes practice, so include plenty of practice time for players to push themselves to quickly read and react to where a fly ball is headed.

As for teaching your players to sprint rather than drift to the ball, younger players often drift while holding their glove out in front of them — thus preventing them from sprinting. Therefore, teach your players to sprint to the ball *as if they did not have a glove.* The glove should come up only right before the catch.

CATCHING (RECEIVING) FLY BALLS

As with receiving ground balls, when receiving fly balls, outfielders should use two hands while following the description provided in the text box on the following page.

Most important, once outfielders are directly under the ball, they should *have their glove slightly to the side (so as to see the ball) and between their nose and the ball.* This puts them in the best position to not only watch the ball into their glove, but also to be ready to transfer the ball to the throwing position. Therefore, during your practice sessions, tell your players repeatedly to keep their glove between their nose and the ball when catching fly balls.

THE THROW

The throw for outfielders is essentially the same as it is for infielders, only the throw is apt to be longer, and the target is likely to change more. To create longer throws with power and speed, have outfielders use a longer follow-through than that used by infielders.

With younger players, all you can hope for is for them to throw the ball to an infielder. With older players, you need to teach them to use good judgment about throwing to the right target, and you need to teach them to throw on a line rather than in a high arching curve that can't be cut off because it is too high. The key here is practicing having infielders and outfielders always knowing the game situation

Sprinting to the ball as if not having a glove and locking in.

Catching with glove between the ball and nose.

Thumbs and Pinkies

Catching balls in the air requires using two hands side by side.

On balls that are above waist level, fielders should use the *thumb-on-thumb* technique. Create the image of touching the thumb of the throwing hand to the thumb of the glove hand in preparation for the ball. True, both thumbs will not be touching, but this image will help fielders get both hands involved in the catch.

On balls below waist level, fielders should use the *pinky-on-pinky* technique. This technique is best for low sinking fly balls or line drives below the belt.

Outfielders Taking a Knee

In the outfield, the central concern should be preventing the ball from going past the outfielder. Outfielders are, after all, the "last line of defense." Therefore, teach outfielders how to take a knee when fielding balls coming to them on the ground. Taking a knee is especially appropriate for those harder hit ground balls into the outfield. It may also be the proper way to teach less advanced outfielders who have a hard time fielding even the slowest of ground balls.

---

and where to throw even before the ball is hit. During practice sessions and while hitting fungos, yell out different game situations before hitting fly balls. That way outfielders and infielders can practice throwing to the correct cut-off man or base.

Glove vs. Elbow

While throwing, some fielders may find it more comfortable to point the glove toward the target instead of pointing the elbow of the lead arm. If one lead arm path isn't working, encourage fielders to experiment with a different lead arm path.

Special Positions

While every fielder needs to know how to field ground balls and throw to a target, catchers and first basemen need to know more.

CATCHERS

The key tasks for catchers are assuming a proper receiving stance, framing pitches so they appear to be strikes, blocking wild pitches, and throwing quickly and on a line to second or third base.

There are two types of receiving stances. The *primary receiving stance* is for when there is no threat of a steal—either because there aren't baserunners or because the rule is no stealing. In the primary receiving stance, the catcher's feet should be slightly bowed outward. Weight should be on the insteps of the feet, and the glove should be slightly extended with the arm relaxed. The target should always be *low*. In this position, the catcher should be comfortable enough to sway from side to side and still easily catch balls.

With runners on base and stealing allowed, catchers should assume the *secondary receiving stance*. This stance is similar to the primary stance, except that the catcher must be ready to catch and throw if a runner attempts a steal. Thus, the catcher should be slightly higher in his squatting position and more on the balls of his feet. However, the glove's position should remain the same, that is, low.

Primary receiving position.

Secondary receiving position.

With respect to framing pitches, teach your catchers to set up and give the pitcher a good low target. Framing also means that when receiving a pitch, catchers should hold strikes still and move balls that are slightly outside the strike zone into the strike zone. This requires receiving the ball by bringing the ball slightly into the body and avoiding stabbing at the ball.

Catchers should not move the glove on balls thrown into the strike zone. Such movement can convince an umpire that the pitch was not a strike. On pitches just outside the strike zone, framing should occur with only a slight movement of the glove or movement of the wrist. For example, catchers should turn the wrist inwards on outside pitches to create an illusion of their being over the plate. There should also be no movement of the body to minimize the appearance of movement and encourage umpires to call strikes. Finally, catchers should not attempt to frame pitches that are clearly outside the strike zone so as to increase the chances of framing succeeding on close pitches.

To block wild throws in the dirt, teach your catchers to quickly read whether or not a pitch is going into the dirt. If so, they should react quickly by going forward, onto the knees, glove on the ground and between the legs, and in a way that prepares the glove and possibly the chest to meet the ball. This is an aggres-

Not framing a pitch.

Framing a pitch.

sive, not passive move — and should be practiced as such. Blocking is as much about desire as it is about technique, so help players take pride in blocking.

As for throwing, the same technique can be used for teaching an infielder how to throw. The only difference is that catchers should bring the ball and glove back to the throwing side ear and only then take the ball from the glove. At that point, the weight should be on the back foot, and the front elbow should be high and pointed at the target. The main effort should be to throw with power and on a direct line to the base where a runner is going.

One last word about coaching young catchers. Stress the importance of being reliable and earning a pitcher's trust that the catcher will catch good pitches, block bad ones,

Blocking a pitch in the dirt.

and quickly get balls back to the pitcher so that he does not lose his rhythm. Stress that winning a pitcher's trust will help a pitcher pitch his best.

FIRST BASEMAN

Three guidelines will help your younger players master playing first base: *Don't hug the bag while in the set*; *don't stretch before the ball is thrown*; *stretch only to receive the ball*.

Younger first basemen are apt to hug or stay too close to the bag for fear of not being able to reach the base in time to receive the throw. However, they need to stay off the bag in order to cover more ground on balls hit their way.

To make their staying off the bag work well, teach your players to look at the bag when a ball is hit, run to the bag, set up, and only then look to the player about to throw to first. In receiving the ball, teach your players to stand square to the player throwing the ball until it is clear where the ball is going. This will allow the first baseman to jump or move quickly to the right or left if a throw is

First baseman too close to bag.

First baseman at right distance from bag.

off line. Once the ball is located and headed the first baseman's way, the first baseman should receive the ball with the glove-side leg stretched out toward the ball and the other leg back and touching the infield side edge of the bag.

Special Situations in Infield Play

There are many special situations in baseball, but only a few have to be taught from the beginning. We believe keeping situational teaching simple is crucial when teaching younger players; with children, the focus should remain on basic mechanics. That said, it is important to teach even younger infielders how to cover a bag to tag out a sliding player and how to execute a rundown. It is important because these two situations occur so frequently and because they can determine the outcome of a game.

First baseman stretching for the throw.

COVERING A BAG

Here, we will focus on covering second base, because that is where covering the bag happens most often. The key is to end up receiving the ball while straddling the bag with the body over the bag but not in the path of the runner so as to avoid injuries. To get to this position of straddling the bag, one technique is to have players first go to the bag and face the fielder who is going to throw the ball. This will allow the player to be in a position to field errant throws.

For throws that are on line to the bag, the player covering the bag should shift to the position of straddling the bag. The body should be bent over, and the glove should receive the ball close to or over the front corner of the base. The player then immediately snaps the glove down to make the tag.

The tag should be quick (tag and pull away)—not just to avoid injury, but also to have a better chance of the runner being called out.

RUNDOWNS

Rundowns occur when a runner is caught between two bases while a player covering one of the bases has the ball. The key to executing a proper rundown is to (1) hold the ball up (for accuracy) to make "dart" throws; (2) minimize the number of throws (to minimize throwing errors); (3) run directly at the runner and make him commit; (4) avoid having a thrown ball hit a runner by

Top and left: Straddling the bag and putting on the tag.

57

establishing a throwing lane (hitting the runner means the runner is given the advanced base); and (5) make it so that if mistakes happen (e.g., a dropped throw), the runner will have to go back to a previous base and not advance.

Most of your instruction should be directed to the infielder with the ball. First, teach your infielders to get the ball to the player covering the advance base so as to set up the run back to the previous base. Second, teach your infielder with the ball to run hard at the runner to make it possible to tag the runner without a throw, and if a throw is needed, to make the distance a short one. Third, teach the player with the ball to move slightly out of the base path in order to watch the glove of the teammate who may be receiving a throw. Doing so will help

In run-downs, hold the ball up and run the runner back to the previous base.

prevent hitting the runner. Fourth, teach the player with the ball to pump fake but not do so too many times — pump faking can cause the ball to come loose and unintentionally fake out the other fielder. Most important, teach the player with the ball to keep the ball up and in his throwing hand as he runs toward the runner, ready to flick the ball to his teammate when the runner commits to retreating to the previous base.

Practice the proper rundown in order to help players get their timing down as well as execute proper rundown mechanics. Proper timing in the rundown refers to throwing at the last second, the moment the runner must commit to retreating to the previous bag and the moment it is clear the runner can't be tagged out with the player holding the ball.

What to Look for When Fielding

Look for positive signs of:

1. An appropriately sized glove.
2. A setting up that includes the "ready" position, a confident-expectant attitude, and possibly the "predatory" step.
3. Attacking the ball in the infield and sprinting after fly balls in the outfield.
4. Receiving line drives and fly balls with the glove and throwing hands in proper position (e.g., between the nose and the ball when catching high fly balls).
5. Receiving ground balls with the glove in front, wide stance, flat back and alligator position.

Keeping an eye on the glove of the teammate who will likely receive a throw in a run-down.

6. Making a smooth transition from receiving to throwing hand.
7. Throwing with the correct alignment of feet and front elbow and with the correct load position for throwing arm ("touch the wall").
8. Proper follow-through on throws with the weight over the front foot.
9. Proper arm position for throwing while running down a baserunner caught in a run-down.
10. Proper set-up for catchers and positioning at first base for first basemen.

Look especially for the following problems:

1. No ready position before the ball is pitched.
2. Staying back on ground balls or breaking late on fly balls (not attacking).

3. Receiving fly balls to the side and ground balls too close to the feet.
4. Throwing without stepping to the target.
5. Throwing without proper load; e.g., quick-arming or not bringing the arm back and up.
6. No follow-through on throws.

3

Pitching

The key to pitching at any level is mental preparation and having the right frame of mind. While fielding and hitting require players to stay relaxed, focused, confident, and aggressive, these requirements are especially needed for pitching. The reasons are obvious. Before every pitch, all eyes are on the pitcher. If the pitcher succeeds, the team is likely to succeed; if the pitcher fails, the team is likely to fail. Pitching, then, is asking a lot of younger players — and so not every child is mentally ready to pitch. We suggest that with younger pitchers you pay special attention to the mental part of the game, to that part that is essential if young pitchers are to succeed.

To do this, you will have to do much more than provide command instructions ("Stay relaxed," "Throw strikes," "Be aggressive," etc.). You will have to help young pitchers focus only on the task and to forget about the batter, the score, and whether fielders make outs or errors. The task is the next pitch, not the previous pitch. The previous pitch doesn't matter. This will be hard for younger pitchers. But if they begin to take pride in focusing on the task, on each and every pitch, they will have learned something central to pitching and will be in a much better position to succeed.

Mechanics of Pitching

With respect to mechanics, the key to pitching is being consistent and maintaining balance throughout the delivery. For younger players, we add that keeping things simple is also crucial — no fancy imitations of major league pitchers are required. Concentrate on helping your pitchers focus on being consistent and maintaining balance throughout the delivery. In reading what follows, we will give you lots of details about pitching. However, the more details you throw at your pitchers, the harder it will be for them to be consistent and maintain balance. Therefore, if you are coaching younger players, you will have to pick and choose so as to keep things simple

SETTING UP TO PITCH

Pitching starts by standing tall and comfortable, with the throwing side foot on the rubber. Standing tall and comfortable (including a slight bend in the knee) not only helps with balance, it also intimidates a batter.

In setting up, we recommend that younger players start with the ball in the glove and the throwing hand holding the ball using the four-seam fastball grip. This is the grip for speed and control. While older players may use different grips to create movement, players younger than fourteen should concentrate on throwing fastballs to keep things simple and, most important, to avoid injury. The bodies of children and young adolescents simply cannot handle the physical strain created by pitches thrown to create movement, such as curveballs.

THE WINDUP

The drop, pivot, and lift comprise the "windup" phase that gets a pitcher into a position to load before delivering the pitch.

The Drop

The drop is the small step backward with the glove side foot. The drop simply gets the body moving. Some pitchers take their drop to the side, some straight back, some at an angle. Whatever the specific direction, it is essential that the pitcher remain in a balanced position, with his weight over the throwing side leg. That is, except for the drop leg, the body should not move behind the rubber.

The Pivot

After the drop, pitchers should pivot their throwing side foot so it is parallel to, in front of, and touching the rubber, allowing the pitcher to then push off of the rubber. As the foot turns, so too does the body, which remains erect ("tall") throughout the

The drop.

pivot. At the conclusion of the pivot, a line drawn through the pitcher's shoulders should point directly to the target.

Also during the pivot, the pitcher should grip the baseball inside the glove, and the glove should be comfortably positioned somewhere in front of and close to the body's midsection. The rest of the body shifts with the pivot foot while the head remains facing the plate and the eyes fixed on the target. At the end of the pivot, the eyes will be looking over the front shoulder and directly at the target.

The Lift

The lift is for helping the body "fall" toward the target during the delivery — much like a platform diver first climbs a platform before diving. After completing the pivot, the glove side knee should come *straight up* to a comfortable level.

How high varies from pitcher to pitcher. Whatever the height, it should be the same every time; consistency is the key. The lift should not involve a kick outwards or inwards, because doing so will put the pitcher in an unbalanced position.

During the lift, the knee reaching its highest point is called the *balance point*, because at the balance point the pitcher needs to be perfectly balanced and ready to drive to the target. Once reaching the balance point, a pitcher should stop momentarily before breaking the hands (the load) and driving to the target (the delivery).

THE LOAD AND DRIVE

In hitting, the load and stride set the stage for the swing. In pitching, the load and drive serve a similar function by setting the stage for the delivery. In both hitting and pitching, you must go back before you go forward, all the while keeping balance and eyes on the target.

The pivot.

Eliminating the Lift

It may help a younger pitcher's development to skip the leg lift and go straight to the load. This is akin to the "slide-step" for more advanced pitchers. Simplifying by eliminating the lift will allow younger players to focus on essential elements of pitching. Later on and after those essential elements are mastered, the lift can be inserted into the routine to add more power.

The Load

Once reaching the balance point position, a pitcher should take the ball out of the glove and break apart the hands with thumbs pointing downward and elbows roughly at shoulder level. As the front or lead leg moves directly toward the target, the hands break downward and then swing up until the arms come level with the shoulders. The pitcher should then be looking directly down the lead arm and at the target. At this point in the delivery, you should be able to draw a line through both arms and see that the line goes directly to the target.

Once the throwing arm is fully extended backward, the throwing hand should be *on top of the ball.* Though this may seem counter-intuitive, having the throwing hand on top of the ball makes it easier to hold the ball than when it is underneath. If you don't believe this, try extending your arm back while holding something heavy with the hand on top and then on the bottom, and you will see what we mean. Furthermore, the hand being on top allows for greater whipping action during the delivery.

The lift.

Looking down the lead arm at the target.

Going Directly to a Raised Forearm Position

Younger pitchers often have problems breaking their hands so that the throwing arm is fully extended backward. With younger pitchers, have them bring their throwing arm back and into a position with the elbow up and the pitching hand on top of the ball facing center field. This will help pitchers reach a good position from which to begin the delivery. Later on, and to get more whip and power into the delivery, a player can adjust and throw using a fully extended arm backward.

The Drive

The purpose of the drive is to shift weight from directly over the back foot to directly over the front foot — so as to set up the delivery. Throughout the drive, the pitcher should remain erect or "tall," with head stationary and eyes fixed on the target. The movement toward the target is a falling movement. Therefore, teach your pitchers to think "*Tall and fall.*"

During the drive and after breaking the hands, the front leg should drive straight at the target until the front foot lands slightly closed; that is, not directly pointing at the target. At the *landing point*, the front leg should be slightly bent, not locked. The back leg should also be bent so as to remain in a position to drive off the rubber. Furthermore, the back leg should not dip down so much as to throw the body off balance.

End of the drive.

THE DELIVERY

At the landing point — and no sooner — the body should naturally begin a torque movement that turns the body into a whip. The throwing arm's forward movement should not begin until the front leg lands. The forearm of the throwing arm rotates inward and up so that it quickly points to the sky with the fingers now behind the ball, and the ball now faces the target. This is the same position that we recommend younger players get into right away instead of extending the throwing arm all the way back. At the top of the throwing arm's path forward, the elbow should be at least as high as the shoulders, and the shoulders should be parallel to the ground.

Throughout the delivery, the front (glove) arm should point directly at the target. Some pitchers like to "throw the glove" at the target. Others like to throw only the front elbow. Whether it is the glove or the elbow that drives the delivery, the key is for the front arm to guide the whole body in a straight-line motion towards the target. To increase torque, at the moment the front foot lands and as the throwing arm whips forward, the glove arm is brought back into the body's midsection.

Beginning of the delivery.

The release point.

Releasing the Ball

At the point of release, the elbow of the throwing arm should be at least parallel with the shoulder. The palm should be under the ball, and the fingers should be behind the ball. The point of release should never occur behind the frame of the body. Ideally, it should occur slightly in front of the body and when the body is perfectly square to the target. To increase whip and avoid shoulder strain, pitchers should whip at both the wrist and elbow.

THE FINISH

In a proper finish, the pitching arm accelerates through the release point and then goes down to finish so that the pitching hand is just outside the front knee. To prevent injury and ensure power, at no point during the finish should the pitching arm be slowed or stopped. The upper body should follow the arm all the way down and into a *"flat back"* position; that is, a position with the back parallel to the ground. Encourage pitchers to *"brush the dirt"* with their throwing hand. This will help them focus on executing a proper finish that ends in a flat back position.

At this point in the delivery, the throwing side leg will naturally be thrust into the air and swing around so as to "plant" in front of the glove side leg. This position is rarely good for fielding, so the pitcher should immediately reposition himself to become ready to field a hit ball.

Focusing on Balance and Direction

With younger players, the focus should remain on achieving a consistent and balanced motion throughout the delivery and finish. It will be too much to expect younger players to follow through and into a flat back position—though you can try. Since younger players do not throw very hard, they won't be injured if they do not follow through into a flat back position. Therefore, don't insist on it. However, do insist on maintaining consistency and balance so that pitchers go straight to the target from the time they start their delivery to the time they finish.

What to Look for When Pitching

The finish.

Look for positive signs of:

1. Being comfortable (loose) and confident.
2. Using a four-seam grip.
3. Maintaining balance: "tall and fall."
4. Maintaining focus on the target.
5. Achieving a good balance point.
6. Breaking hands down and into the proper position to begin the delivery.
7. Starting the delivery when the front, lead foot lands.
8. Achieving a good release point.
9. Having a full follow-through.

Look especially for the following problems:

1. Being tight and nervous.
2. Losing balance during the pivot, load, delivery, or follow-through.
3. Moving forward in a direction other than straight to the target.
4. Taking the eyes off the target.
6. Releasing the ball behind the body rather than out in front.
7. Failing to follow through.
8. Ending the follow-through in an open or too closed a position.

Key Concepts

- Get comfortable (loose)
- Tall and fall
- Maintain a focus on the target
- Balance point
- Breaking the hands
- Hand on top of the ball
- Straight line (to the target)
- Torque
- Elbow at least parallel with shoulder
- Plant closed
- Release point
- Flat back finish

Part Two

Managing Practices and Games

In the section on teaching baseball mechanics, the main theme was explaining so children can understand. In this section on managing practices and games, while the theme of explaining is continued, other themes take over, such as the themes of being organized and helping children manage their emotions. However, with the introduction of new themes, there remains the overarching message that managing means something different from managing older players when the task is to manage children.

When the task is to manage children, there is more to managing practices and games than attending to baseball mechanics, baseball strategies, and winning. There is also matching how one manages to the needs of children.

4

Managing Practices[*]

In the chapters on teaching baseball mechanics, the focus was on explaining and demonstrating so children understand. Here, the focus shifts to helping players learn new skills and practice proper mechanics so that what gets practiced becomes committed to muscle memory.

Practice Sessions

Practice sessions also help players use proper mechanics when playing real games, either by the way drills are *packaged* or by having players practice in *game-like* situations. Doing so is essential because players can demonstrate proper mechanics during drills focusing on component skills, yet play poorly once the games begin. Here, we will suggest an approach to managing practices that helps children practice as they would play in real games.

Finally, good practice sessions develop not just technical skills (good mechanics) but tactical skills as well. Tactical skills have to do with "reading" game situations and making good decisions, particularly decisions about when and where to run and when and where to throw.

Practice sessions also shift the focus to figuring out how best to motivate players to give up bad ways, such as "stepping in the bucket" when hitting, short-arming when throwing, and drifting rather than sprinting to catch fly balls, and to adopt good ways and proper mechanics. As mentioned before, we strongly advocate your not relying too much on command instructions ("Run hard," "Get in the ready position," etc.) to motivate players. Instead, we advocate your thinking about motivating players using a variety of positive methods and practice session features, including your being organized, finding ways to keep every child active, providing drills and equipment that reduce the fear factor, and providing

Authors' Note: Chapter Four was co-authored by Cara Hovhanessian.

72

fun and meaningful games. However, the single most important method for motivating may well be the way you provide feedback.

PROVIDING FEEDBACK

The practice makes permanent observation suggests it is essential that you give players constant feedback — to ensure that they aren't practicing bad mechanics but also to ensure they know how to make corrections and practice the skills they need. However, to give good feedback, you have to know what to assess, what to comment on as well as what not to comment on, and how to explain so children will understand and feel supported. Giving feedback is no easy task. To make the task easier, we break it down into the following short list of suggestions. In giving feedback:

1. *Match the detail given in your feedback to a player's age and level of ability.* Beginners need only "rough" feedback. Giving lots of details to beginners can easily overwhelm. For example, if a child is just learning to hit, it might be enough to focus on a child getting into a proper stance and swinging down and through the ball. Details having to do with hip rotation and follow-through can come later.

2. *Explain so children can understand.* This means avoiding giving explanations that require thinking about more than one relationship at a time and using clear images whenever you can (see introduction for more discussion).

3. *Encourage and challenge.* Despite the myths about great coaches being tough guys, the fact is that the vast majority of great coaches are great because they know how to teach, encourage, and challenge. Teaching is covered by the first two suggestions. Encouraging and challenging is covered by this suggestion. To encourage and challenge is different than to praise. To encourage and challenge is to focus more on *process* than on achievement. ("I see you starting to swing down and through the ball. Now really concentrate on swinging through the ball so you hit those two imaginary balls that follow.") Furthermore, to encourage and challenge is to help players go to the next level or take the next step — and to communicate clearly that you know they can. Therefore, when encouraging and challenging, you communicate to players that they are improving and that improving is what you expect.

4. *Be positive not just with words but also with facial expression, tone of voice, and body posture.* This last suggestion may be the most important. While college and professional players sometimes say things like "If coach doesn't yell at you, he doesn't care about you" and believe what they say, younger players usually react

quite negatively to coaches yelling at them or otherwise providing feedback in negative ways. It may not show up in the short term, but in the long term it shows up in players expressing resentment over how they were treated and in their quitting before they would naturally stop participating in organized (coached) baseball. But even if there are no obvious negative outcomes, yelling at children or otherwise giving constant negative feedback can't help but undermine the goal of children developing a love for the game. So disabuse yourself of any thoughts about children needing you to be tough. Besides, baseball is a game that requires players to relax. Who can relax when being yelled at?

A coach's job is to be positive — and not just with words (photograph by Jay Reichheld).

EQUIPMENT

Throughout this discussion of managing practices, we will assume you have only limited resources for buying equipment other than the usual equipment issued to Little League teams — bats, baseballs, helmets, bases, and catcher's equipment. With regard to extra equipment, we suggest you bring the following:

1. Rag balls, or if rag balls are too expensive, then tennis balls, which are especially good for reducing the fear factor during fielding drills. Rag balls are better than tennis balls because they simulate the feel, movement, and even weight of baseballs. (Note: Yellow rag balls are easier to find in the woods!)

2. At least one batting tee, preferably several, which are good for batting drills. Even the pros rely on batting tees.

3. Small plastic cones, which are good for baserunning drills and for creating games for practicing specific skills.

Extra equipment for practice sessions.

4. Tape balls, balls made of masking tape made into a ball no bigger than a golf ball, which are good for hitting drills and getting players to watch the ball.

Explaining and Demonstrating What Needs to be Practiced

One last introductory note: Before beginning drills and practice games, you should explain and demonstrate the skills to be practiced by following the suggestions in the introduction and in the previous section on teaching baseball mechanics. If the skill is a new skill, with younger players you can lead them by going through the motions of executing the skill properly. One way to do this is to have players in rows behind you and imitating you as you go through the skill. For example, to demonstrate how to throw a baseball, you can have players imitate how you are throwing (without a ball) as you go through the throwing motions slowly and with your back to your players.

However, what is most important when introducing a new skill is to give players just enough information for them to be able to roughly approximate what you show them. They need not get it right the first time a skill is explained and demonstrated. That is what drills are for — getting it right.

Drills*

Drills are a necessary part of any practice. They ensure that players understand and practice good mechanics, and they help players commit good mechanics to muscle memory. Regardless of age, drills are primarily for practicing component skills, such as practicing the follow-through at the very end of throw-

*See Appendix A for more drills.

ing a baseball. However, if players do nothing more than practice component skills separately, they may never be able to put all the component skills together to become accomplished players. There are, for example, many young players who look great during a soft toss drill designed to help them swing down and through the ball but then swing poorly during real games.

PACKAGING DRILLS

To solve this problem of connecting individual drills to performing well in real games, you need to *package* drills so that they fit together and help players practice under near-game conditions. Here are two suggestions for packaging drills.

1. *Package drills as a backward progression or chain for combining component skills.* As we have said many times, fielding, hitting, baserunning, and pitching should be thought of as complex skills made up of several component skills. And component skills are best practiced both separately and together. But how?

One good way is to package drills so that they progressively lead backward from the end of a complex skill to the beginning, what we will refer to as *backward chaining*. Some complex skills such as hitting do not lend themselves to this method, but others such as throwing and pitching do lend themselves.

Using the example of throwing, here is what backward chaining looks like as a series of drills to practice throwing a baseball properly:

1. One-knee, break, freeze, and throw drill: While on their throwing side knee and facing a partner several yards away, have players throw to their partner. In this drill, players start with the ball and glove near the chest, and on your command, they "break" hands and go into the load position (throwing hand facing away from the partner, "touching the wall" and lead arm elbow "sighting the target") and then "freeze" so you can check for proper positioning of arms and hands. Then when you instruct them to throw, players complete the delivery, concentrating on providing an over-the-top release and a good follow through,

Above and following page: Start of backward chaining drill on throwing.

with chest ending up over the front knee.

2. Same drill as before except players start from a standing position closed to the target. Go through the same "break and freeze" routine as before.

3. Same drill as before except players take one side step toward the target before throwing to include footwork in the entire throwing sequence.

You'll note that in this backward chaining way of practicing throwing, players end up throwing as they should throw in a real game while using all the various component skills in throwing.

2. *Package drills as a forward progression or chain for eventually playing under game conditions.* Backward chaining helps combine component skills. However, what we are left with is a player performing a complex skill but not under game conditions. To progress toward game conditions, drills can also be packaged to increasingly approximate game conditions. For example, drills can be performed at increasingly faster speed until the rate required is game speed. Similarly, drills can be performed under increasingly competitive conditions until the competition level is that of the real game. To illustrate, here is a sequence of throwing drills:

1. Have players form groups of three, with each threesome spread out in a line and with the lines parallel to one another. Players in each threesome should be about fifteen yards apart. The middle player serves as the cut-off man, and the outside players serve as the outfielder and player covering a base respectively. The first drill is at half speed. Have players simply throw to one another, with the end players always throwing to the middle and aiming for the chest.

2. Same drill as before but at full speed.

3. Same drill as before but each group competes with one another to see how many rounds with accurate throws they can complete within a 30-second period.

You'll note that as was the case with the example of backward chaining, this example of forward chaining is all about progressing toward playing as one should play in real games.

DRILLS FOR CORRECTING NATURALLY OCCURRING PROBLEMS

Any drill that teaches and reinforces good mechanics will also be a drill that corrects for *naturally occurring problems*. For example, in the throwing drills just discussed, your checking for proper follow-through will help correct a common problem among beginners, namely, short-arming or failing to follow through.

However, some naturally occurring problems require special treatment because they become habitual and/or because they are constantly being reinforced by their solving some problem, such as being afraid of getting hurt. Stepping in the bucket while hitting and catching balls to the side are prime examples, so we can use these to illustrate drills for correcting naturally occurring problems.

To correct the problem of stepping in the bucket, one simple drill is to place a bat on the ground and pointed directly ahead as well as just behind the batter. If a batter steps back while hitting, he will step on the bat; that should be enough to remind him not to step in the bucket. If it isn't, another drill can be used, one requiring a batter to hit with both feet standing in tires. The tires will prevent any movement backward.

To correct the naturally occurring problem of catching thrown balls to the side, you can use rag or tennis balls during fielding drills until players become competent enough to use real baseballs. Furthermore, you can have players catch softly thrown baseballs with their two bare hands. Catching with bare hands encourages players to catch with both hands out in front of the chest.

One naturally occurring problem when hitting involves players opening up their front shoulder too soon because they constantly try to pull the ball. To correct this naturally occurring problem, and to encourage players to hit through the ball rather than trying to pull the ball, you can have players hitting balls off a batting tee placed well in front of them. At first they are likely to miss, but eventually they will get the hang of hitting through the ball.

Other naturally occurring problems include not attacking the ball when

fielding grounders, lunging when hitting, slowing down before reaching first base when running, and keeping arms and elbows too low during the load and delivery phases when pitching. Each of these can be corrected using drills targeted to correct them. Use the drills focusing on naturally occurring problems whenever the usual teaching drills aren't enough to break bad habits.

To emphasize hitting through the ball, have players hit off a batting tee placed out in front.

Taking a Games Approach*

We've been discussing how to package drills so that players progress toward playing the way they should play during real games. However, taking a games approach implies more. Specifically, a games approach implies *shaping* the game of baseball, *focusing* players' attention on some particular point or skill, and *enhancing* play so as to motivate players to practice what needs to be practiced. We can see how shaping, focusing, and enhancing work using a single example of a game designed to help players when hitting make contact and hit line drives up the middle.

Initially players will miss, but eventually they will learn how to hit through the ball.

SHAPING

Shaping play usually means one or more of the following: changing a

See Appendix Two for more games for practicing.

rule, changing the number of players, changing the equipment, changing the size or shape of the playing area, or changing the playing goal. Whatever the change, it should help players focus on some important point or skill needed to play baseball — such as the point that trying to hit line drives up the middle leads to more successful hitting than trying for big hits by pulling the ball. For beginning players especially, trying to pull the ball often leads to opening up the front shoulder too soon and taking the eyes off the ball, resulting in lots of strikeouts.

To get players to concentrate on hitting the ball up the middle, one can first *shape* play by bringing the foul lines in toward second base so that the foul lines go through where the shortstop and second baseman normally play. With such a playing field, hitters can succeed only by hitting up the middle.

FOCUSING

You can shape how baseball is normally played, and players still might not get the point. Therefore, you need also to help players *focus* on whatever it is they need to learn. If it is hitting up the middle, then you need to stop play to demonstrate just how this is done, why it should be done and what happens when play-

A game for hitting up the middle.

ers try to pull the ball. In other words, you must focus your players' attention on why and how to hit for contact and up the middle as well as on why and how failing to do so often leads to problems.

In getting players to focus, perhaps you start them hitting off a tee and then progress to their hitting live pitching. Perhaps you help them focus by stopping the practice game whenever they try to pull the ball — to show them how they can do better. Whatever the method, you should constantly support their getting the point and their acting on the point.

ENHANCING PLAY

Shaping and focusing are the essential ingredients in a games approach to managing baseball practices. However, there is a third ingredient referred to as *enhancing* play. You can enhance play by presenting unusual challenges and rewards that make your point stand out and become more likely to be followed. In the example of hitting up the middle game, you can say, "If you hit the pitcher's mound or second base, it's a home run." Then divide your team into two teams and have them compete against one another.

Organizing Practices

To organize a practice means to organize time, materials, players and coaches. Organizing time refers to the practice schedule. Organizing materials means having the necessary equipment and directions for when and how equipment gets used and put away. Organizing players and coaches means organizing them into groups. Some would add monitoring to this list of what organizing refers to since you will need to figure out how players can be constantly monitored to ensure that they are practicing good mechanics. However, regardless of the kind of organization, your organizing should always aim to ensure that everyone is actively engaged and practicing all the time.

Here are suggestions for organizing practices:

1. *At the beginning of practices, meet with your players to forecast what will be happening during the practice session and what rules or procedures they will need to follow to ensure safety, their focusing on practicing good mechanics, and their making smooth transitions from one part of practice to another.*

2. *Focus on fundamentals.* Developing baseball skills takes years, not months, so never think that you should move off of focusing on fundamentals. Even if

players have been playing youth baseball for several years, they still need to practice the fundamentals involved in fielding, hitting, baserunning and pitching. Many big leaguers do the same.

3. *Begin practice sessions with monitored catch and throw.* Catch and throw between pairs of players is a good way to warm up. Furthermore, if monitored, catch and throw can serve the additional purpose of practicing the fundamentals in catching and throwing properly.

4. *Divide practice sessions into stations.* In order to have everyone engaged all the time, divide your team into three or more groups stationed in different areas of the field.

5. *For at least a portion of your practices, have your pitchers practicing pitching to one another* by doing specific drills, such as one-knee drills to accentuate the follow-through, and drills to strengthen the throwing arm, such as the long toss drill.

6. *In the infield, create different stations depending on the drill or practice game.* One day you might have a station to practice run-downs. Another day, you might

Team meetings before and after games can do much to establish a good frame of mind (photograph by Jay Reichheld).

During practices, set up stations where small groups can practice specific skills (photograph by Jay Reichheld).

use the entire infield to practice fielding ground balls. The nature of the infield station depends, therefore, on the nature of the skill being practiced and on what you have decided is the most pressing need.

7. *Have a separate station for outfield play.* Here is where you have players practice sprinting to fly balls, catching balls with the glove between the ball and nose, and taking a knee on hard-hit ground balls. These and other skills are central to good outfield play.

8. *Plan so that players are monitored all the time.* Even if a station does not have an adult at the station, you can still monitor players from afar. For example, if pitchers are off by themselves practicing their follow-through, you can communicate from afar how they are doing and give encouragement for them to practice in the right way.

9. *Throughout the entire practice session, set the right tone and energy level in the way you communicate and behave.* Ideally, your positive tone and energy should establish a relaxed and positive atmosphere, and one that also energizes your players.

10. *End practice sessions with a group meeting that marks what players have accomplished and forecasts what players can expect during games and future practice sessions.*

One final word about managing practices: There are designated practice sessions and there are pre-game warm-up sessions that usually last less than an hour. For younger players especially, the pre-game warm-up sessions should also be thought of as practice sessions — times when players should be monitored to practice good mechanics. Therefore, *teach your players to see pre-game warm-ups as practice sessions.*

5

Managing Games

In high school, college, and the pros, a coach good at managing games is someone who knows how to win. However, the situation is quite different when managing games played by children. The reason is that children are less concerned about winning and more concerned about participating and having a quality experience that includes high drama, personal achievement, and being with friends. Therefore, when managing the games of children, the main question is *"How can you manage games to keep the team competitive while also ensuring a quality experience for each and every child?"*

In other words, to manage games played by children is to manage a dilemma. This means that if you are doing a good job, you will always feel yourself engaged in a balancing act, balancing the needs of individual players to enjoy themselves and develop a love for the game and the need to keep the team competitive.

Positioning Players and Making Up Batting Lineups

Because managing a dilemma is hard and sometimes unsatisfying, there will be temptations to abandon the task and go flat out for winning games. The first of these temptations occurs before the games begin. It is the temptation to field only the best team and to send to bat only the best hitters. Of course, league rules will prevent you from giving into this temptation entirely — but they may not prevent you from effecting compromises that make playing baseball less enjoyable for the less skilled players and that undermine the goal of helping them love the game. Here, we need to help you resist this temptation even while we help you field a competitive team.

With regard to positioning players, you can field a competitive team while still giving your least skilled players the opportunity to play desirable infield positions. You can do this by first understanding that at the youngest levels (when stealing isn't allowed) there really are only three key positions where you must have skilled players in order for your team to remain competitive — and also for preserving the integrity of the game. The key positions are pitcher, first base, and shortstop.

Having a pitcher who can throw strikes is essential, not just for being competitive but also for keeping the game interesting for everyone involved. Nothing saps energy from a game and turns the game into something other than baseball more than when a pitcher walks batter after batter.

The games also need a first baseman who can catch balls even if they are slightly off target. If the first baseman can't do this, the game becomes a game of errors. As for shortstop, because the shortstop will likely be in on more plays than any other infielder except the first baseman and needs to make the long throw to first, it is also essential to have a reliable shortstop.

This leaves two infield positions, second and third base, that you can use to rotate less skilled players in and out of, leaving plenty of flexibility for satisfying everyone's desire to play the infield. Furthermore, in doing so, no player gets stigmatized; that is, no player gets labeled as the player who can't play the infield.

As for catcher, at the youngest ages, catchers need to receive and quickly throw the ball back to the pitcher so that the pitcher maintains rhythm. For this position, we recommend that you choose players who can commit to taking care of the pitcher's need to maintain rhythm. Those players need not be highly skilled, but they do need to be motivated to take care of the pitcher. Of course, when stealing is allowed, you need a catcher who can make the throw to second.

When rotating players in and out of the outfield, think in terms of threesomes, with the center fielder always being the best of the three. And avoid assigning the same players to play right field since right field can sometimes stigmatize a player.

With regard to batting lineups, when quality of experience for each player is your aim, there really isn't an ideal batting lineup. However, whatever order you choose, you must manage the dilemma between keeping players reasonably happy and keeping the team competitive — and this means you cannot always stick the worst hitters at the end of the lineup.

Consider bunching your five best hitters in the middle of the lineup so as to maximize the possibility of your team having a couple of high-scoring innings. Then, all you have to do is alternate the batting order from one game to the next, going from first to last one game, last to first the next game, and so forth. That way no one will get stigmatized by being stuck at the bottom of the order, and in any given game, your best hitters will get to bat often enough.

This method of determining a batting lineup isn't the only method that will keep the focus on ensuring quality experience for all players while also keeping the team competitive. There are other methods that may work equally well or better. Use them if they seem better for your team. However, keep in mind that "better" is never to be defined only in terms of winning but also in terms of which method better ensures a quality experience for each and every player.

With players 12 years and older, you can start to field teams and make up batting lineups more on the basis of ability; however, these older players need and deserve to participate in a substantial portion of each game. We will have more to say about this later on in the concluding remarks when we take up the question of values in more depth.

One more suggestion related to positioning players: In every inning when your team is in the field, you will have scheduled several players to be on the bench. Have one of these players be among the more skilled on the team so as to avoid having an inning where all your most skilled players are on the bench, thus risking having an inning when the game in the field falls apart. Also, if a player is scheduled to pitch the next inning, have that player be on the bench the inning before so as to provide the player with time to warm up.

Pre-Game Practice Sessions

As mentioned at the end of Chapter Five, the time prior to games should be thought of as time to practice. With this in mind, you should oversee these pre-game practice sessions, keeping aware that "practice makes permanent."

By saying you should think of pre-game sessions as practice sessions, we don't mean you should be introducing new drills and practice games. Rather, we mean that during pre-game sessions, you should be monitoring players to see that they are throwing, fielding and batting using good mechanics from the moment they step onto the field to play catch and throw.

Playing catch and throw to open pre-game practice sessions should also include players throwing ground balls to one another as well as throwing long toss. (See Appendix A for a description of long toss.) We especially recommend long toss for those who will be pitching to help pitchers stretch their arm muscles and adopt a mind-set that is helpful for pitching. There is nothing quite like long toss to help a player focus on the process of pitching and adopt the mind-set of a pitcher.

At some point during pre-game practice sessions, you and your assistant should hit ground balls and fly balls to your players who should be rotating

It is common for players to warm up using poor mechanics (photograph by Jay Reichheld).

between infield and outfield in order to help them get used to the eye-hand coordination needed to field and give players feedback on their mechanics. In addition, players should be rotating in and out of a soft-toss station or station with a tee, where they can practice hitting balls (rag or tennis balls) into a batting screen — ideally, with someone there to monitor their mechanics.

Right before the games begin, post the batting lineup and each inning's assignments in the field so that players know beforehand what to expect. Doing so will free up players to focus on playing the game. This is also a time when you can encourage players to prepare themselves mentally by using the imagery exercises that you have taught them during practice sessions. (See the next chapter for details.)

Managing Attention and Focus

Younger players are famous for losing attention and focus, so much so that they can momentarily forget they are playing in a game. This is natural for many,

Post lineups before games so everybody knows where they are supposed to be (photograph by Jay Reichheld).

so don't make a moral issue out of a player not paying attention. Rather, support each and every player's ongoing efforts to pay attention and keep focus. This means you need to find ways to help your players pay attention and keep focus on their own by using positive methods.

When players lose focus, such as looking down at the ground while in the outfield, yell out positive code words such as "turbo" and "supercharge," words the players experience as positive reminders that they need to focus on the game. Also, assign an infielder the role of calling out the situation. For example, if you see your outfielders gazing off into the distance, yell out to the designated infielder a pre-arranged code word such as "situation"—some word that indicates the player is to relay to the others what the situation is ("Man on first, two outs," "Man on first and third, nobody out" and so forth). Doing so will keep players "in the game" and give players a sense of being in control.

Paying attention takes a different meaning when a child has a diagnosed disorder having to do with attention, such as attention deficit with hyperactivity disorder (ADHD). Don't worry about the disorder—the last thing a child needs is

> ### *When Attention Is Not on the Game*
>
> While playing right field during a game of rather great importance, Connor became engaged in deep observation of the grass in his immediate area. The first batter of the inning hit a pop fly that headed directly at Connor. Realizing the player was paying absolutely no attention to the game, his coach shrieked, "Connor! Heads up!" Connor threw his head up in the direction of his coach and began to sprint, without purpose, toward the dugout. The ball landed perfectly inside the patch of grass that he had been so intensively studying just seconds before, and the batter proceeded to jog around the bases for an inside-the-park home run. Connor stopped at the pitcher's mound looking confused as the other team embraced their hero for having scored the go-ahead run.

to be defined by his or her disorder. Do worry about giving extra positive support for that child, support completely devoid of moralizing and negative judgments. Children with attention-related disorders can't help themselves and should be given more positive support, not less, to help them perform at their best. Sometimes that support will mean going far beyond doing what you think is reasonable, as indicated in the following example.

> ### *Giving Extra Support for Players with Attention Problems*
>
> Max had serious problems paying attention to coaches' instructions. Once after he had reached first base with two out in the last inning of a game his team was losing by three runs, the coach yelled over that he was not to try to steal because the team needed more than a run to tie. On the first pitch, Max refrained from stealing, but on the second pitch, he took off. He was out by a mile. Game over.
>
> Getting up from the ground, he turned sheepishly to the coach, realizing what he had done. However, the coach knew that Max had simply lost track of the instruction not to steal. Instead of criticizing Max, the coach apologized for not reminding him before the second pitch. Max looked up appreciatively. In fact, the coach was right to apologize, since Max really did need that extra reminder.

How you position young players will often have a significant influence on how well they pay attention and keep focus. Ironically, it is often the players who have the most difficulty paying attention and keeping focus that get assigned to the positions where it is most difficult to pay attention and maintain focus — those positions being in the outfield. Here is an example of a coach using positioning to help a child keep his focus.

Using Positioning to Manage Attention Problems

Taylor, age nine, had severe attention problems. When positioned in the outfield, he inevitably had difficulty paying attention—a passing airplane, some comment shouted out by a parent in the stands, a beetle landing on a blade of grass, anything and everything was apt to take his attention away from focusing on the game.

To remedy this situation, the coach assigned Taylor to play catcher. There, Taylor had much less difficulty paying attention and focusing on the game. Not only were there people all around him reminding him that a game was being played, the fact that pitches were being thrown directly at him ensured he had no choice but to pay attention to the game. Since there was no stealing allowed in this league of nine-year-olds, Taylor did just fine.

In sum, one of your more important considerations when managing the games of young children is how to help them pay attention and keep focus. You can do so using a variety of methods, but whatever the method, it should be positive, not negative.

Managing Pitchers

There is no more important task during games than that of managing pitchers. Everything hinges on pitchers maintaining the integrity of the game by consistently getting the ball over the plate. You need to select pitchers who show promise for being able to consistently get the ball over the plate.

However, getting the ball over the plate may not happen during pressure moments or when something happens to frustrate a pitcher, such as an error by an infielder and a bad call by an umpire. At those times, your pitchers may need your help to calm themselves and keep their focus on pitching. Give them that help but only after carefully assessing what is helpful for different pitchers. Some respond positively to your giving advice; some do not. Some are helped by trips to the mound; some are not. Don't think when helping pitchers calm themselves and regain focus that one size fits all.

That said, almost any child pitcher is apt to respond positively to humor, as exemplified in the following:

A Little Humor to Calm a Pitcher

During one inning in a game between nine-year-olds and after several hits and a couple of runs scored, the pitcher began to cry. The coach trotted out to the mound looking calm and upbeat. With a hand on the pitcher's shoulder, he asked with a serious expression on his face, "Do you remember what's the most important thing about playing baseball?" Since in practice sessions the coach had taught the players the answer, the pitcher gained composure and said with a smile, "No picking your nose." "That's right," said the coach, and the two of them laughed. When the inning resumed, the pitcher had no difficulty ending the inning with no additional runs scored.

By distracting anxious and frustrated pitchers with humor, you help them get beyond their anxiety and frustration so that they can get back to focusing on pitching.

Managing pitchers also requires knowing when and how to replace a pitcher who is struggling so much that the game is in jeopardy of getting out of hand. The key here is your having gone over during practice sessions how pitchers should react to being replaced in the middle of an inning.

During these practice sessions, you need to get each and every pitcher to buy into the philosophy that, in being pulled, pitchers need not, indeed should not, feel they have failed or feel shame. Rather, they should feel that pitching is a team effort. Remind them that even Hall of Fame professional pitchers get replaced in the middle of innings. And remind them, too, that after being pulled in one game, they will have plenty of opportunities in the future to pitch again and show they can pitch through even the most pressured and frustrating moments in a game. Have them set that as their goal. In other words, when you walk to the mound to replace a pitcher, your pitcher should already have internalized a mental attitude and philosophy that you have instilled in practice sessions and allows a pitcher to give up the mound with grace.

To be a pitcher requires special ability to stay confident and focused (photograph by Jay Reichheld).

Of course, when managing the games of children, tears happen. When they do, provide an arm around the shoulder, sympathetic words, and a forecast of better games to come. And with children, there are also times when a player will tell you in his own indirect way that he has had enough. You need to learn to listen and follow his lead; there will be plenty of opportunities later on to help the player become more mentally tough, as discussed in the next chapter. On the following page is one such example of a player saying in his own way that he had had enough:

One final word about managing pitchers and preventing overuse injuries. Your league is apt to have strict rules about when and for how long you can keep a player pitching; there may be limits on pitch count. The league rules are what you will be using to prevent overuse injuries. If you aren't in a league with such rules, you need to use good sense, because over-pitching a child or young adolescent can do permanent harm. The key is not having a pitcher pitch too many innings while allowing for several days rest between games.

Strange Medical Problems on the Mound

One eight-year-old pitcher was having a particularly difficult time throwing strikes in the first inning. He also gave up a couple of hits. Coming in from the field following the inning, he proceeded to explain to the coach that his arm was hurting. The coach, thinking that muscle soreness or fatigue was the issue, asked him to explain the details of his ailment. The pitcher indicated that he received a vaccination two days prior to the game and, even though the shot was in his left (non-throwing) arm, it had "migrated over" to the right arm and was now causing him discomfort. He even showed the Band-Aid to prove it.

Managing Situations

Most of the time, the games simply play themselves out according to the rules and how pitchers are pitching, fielders are fielding, and hitters are hitting. Most of the time, there aren't many decisions for a coach to make; the decisions that really matter have occurred prior the games, such as positioning and batting lineups.

However, there are certain situations when it is wise to intervene, make some decision, and communicate that decision to your players — all for the sake of keeping your team competitive. These situations include when runners are on first and third with stealing allowed, and when games are tied in the late innings.

Your decisions will have to do with risk management and assessing how skilled your players are at hitting, fielding, and pitching. There are general guidelines to follow. Here are a couple having to do with offense:

• *Have batters "take" the pitch (not swing) on a 3–0 count.* Many younger players need to be reminded to not swing at a 3–0 count. We also recommend you remind them to fake the bunt on a 3–0 count, something that needs to be practiced.

• *With runners on first and third, have the runner on first steal on the first pitch.* This guideline obviously doesn't apply if there is a no stealing rule. Nor does it apply if your team is behind by several runs in the late innings when the runs scored by the runners on base won't be the deciding runs. However, when stealing is allowed, most of the time it does apply because the opposing team rarely attempts to throw out the runner at second, and if an attempt is made, the runner on third can score. If you would like to get fancy, instruct the runner on first to briefly delay stealing second (or pretend to fall down) so as to draw the throw. But to pull this off, you will have to practice it before games.

• *If stealing is allowed, do not allow runners to steal if it is late in the game and the team is behind by several runs.* The reason for this guideline should be obvious. When more runs need to be scored than there are runners on base, it makes no sense to risk having a runner thrown out, especially at the younger levels when making double plays is so rare.

As for guidelines having to do with defense, here are a couple:

• *Have players make the sure out.* This guideline applies especially in the games of younger players when outs are often more important than runs. Therefore, if a runner is going from third to home after the batter has hit a grounder to shortstop, most of the time the shortstop should be throwing to first to get the sure out. If the shortstop is about to throw home, you will have to yell out that he is to throw to first.

• *Move infielders and outfielders in when it is crucial to prevent a runner on base from scoring.* This guideline applies to late innings when there is a runner on third with less than two outs and the game might be decided by one run.

Aside from implementing these guidelines, you will occasionally want to move your outfielders so that they are better positioned for particular batters and certain situations. And, of course, your base coaches will be telling baserunners when they should slide, hold up, or go for an extra base.

Other than these guidelines and situations calling for you to insert yourself directly into the games, you should keep the decision-making in the hands of the players; otherwise, the players will feel over-controlled, not a feeling conducive to having fun.

CALLING TIME-OUTS

At the younger levels, there are added reasons for calling time-outs. First, younger players can become so anxious or overwhelmed that they become incapable of playing the game. A time-out for a conference with an anxious hitter can do lots to calm his nerves and get him back to taking pleasure in hitting a baseball (or at least trying to do so), especially when what you say to a hitter is slightly humorous, clever, or simply encouraging. And there are times when younger players become overwhelmed and need your help to regain control and pull themselves back together, as illustrated in the following example.

Sometimes Meltdowns Occur

Joey, an eleven-year-old, was usually the team's leader by example because of his hard-nosed style of play and mature decision-making. But his desire to win would sometimes get the best of him. After grounding out in a pivotal game to end the inning, Joey "lost it" and threw his helmet halfway across the field. Not knowing how else to release his anger (he looked like he was genuinely about to burst), Joey stormed past his dugout and plopped down behind a large oak tree. Tears of rage and frustration streamed down his face as he wallowed in his self-pity.

Another reason for calling time-outs in games for young players is that younger players can be easily confused when trying to read signs or follow verbal instructions being given from afar. A time-out can clear up the confusion.

We recommend that you make judicious use of time-outs whenever you sense a player is overly anxious, losing control, or is confused. However, we don't recommend that you call so many time-outs that you undermine the rhythm and quality of the game. Though time-outs are necessary on occasion, they don't add to the excitement and fun of playing the game.

Signs

During games there are several situations where you may want to employ signs, even with younger players. This is particularly true in situations calling for a bunt or steal, or if your team is in the field, for a particular reaction to a bunt or steal. However, there is another reason we recommend the occasional use of signs with even younger players. Signs can add fun and excitement to a game.

With younger players, we recommend the simplest of signs, those created by touching parts of the body such as the arm or particular clothing items such as the hat. For example, touching either arm could always mean steal. Touching the hat could always mean bunt.

If the league allows for steals, decide whether to teach your players to fake the bunt when they are at bat when another player on base is given the steal sign. This is a bit complicated for children younger than twelve, so you might want to reserve this wrinkle for teams with players older than eleven.

As for signs meant to direct fielders how to react to bunts and steals, the general rule is to be conservative when managing the games of young children. For example, being conservative is to use signs for *not* trying to throw a runner out

Calling a time-out with runners on first and third.

who is likely to steal second. This is an especially important sign for when there are runners at first and third — when even an accurate throw to second is likely to result in the runner on third coming home. During practice sessions, you can decide whether the catcher is to throw the ball back to the pitcher or to the shortstop who has come in a few steps toward home and is in an excellent position to throw out the runner on third should he be trying to steal home.

Managing Toxic Influences

Another major difference between managing the games of high school, college, and professional players and managing the games of children is that when managing the games of children you need to manage the toxic influences that occur when adults get angry, when parents coach from the sidelines, and when opposing coaches or umpires ignore or do a poor job of assessing the needs of children. For children, these can ruin the experience of playing baseball, which is why we call them "toxic."

BACKGROUND ANGER

The anger adults sometimes express during games includes anger expressed by coaches, umpires, and parents. Regardless of where the anger comes from, the effect of this "background anger," as it is referred to in the literature (Omli and LaVoi, 2008) is almost always negative, something that works against children having fun and loving the game.

Your job is to manage adult anger by doing what you can to prevent it from occurring in the first place, and when it occurs, doing what you can to keep it brief and not so damaging. In the next chapter, we discuss *reframing,* a method for keeping your relationships with players positive, even when they mess up or misbehave. Reframing is a method for preventing your own anger from creating a negative climate during the game. With umpires, if and when umpires make bad calls, reframe the situation as a positive opportunity to model for your players how to voice disagreement without showing anger. Again, the evidence shows that children will notice and appreciate your not making a moral issue out of a blown call (Nucci, 2001).

However, there are other reasons for controlling your anger with umpires. After an umpire has made a bad call, if you control your anger and simply *mark* what you think was the correct call, later in the game you are more likely to find the umpire giving your team a *make-up call*, a call in your team's favor when it may not be the right call.

With parents, you can do a lot to prevent background anger by holding pre-season meetings and by providing pre-season communications that explain the concept of background anger and its negative effects. If and when a parent yells and directs anger toward a player, coach, or umpire, find a way to tactfully communicate that you need parental support to keep adult anger out of the games. You don't have to have face-to-face meetings with the offending parent. Often, you can get the job done by communicating (for example, via e-mail) to all your parents, reminding them of the pre-season discussions about eliminating background anger during games.

PARENTS COACHING FROM THE SIDELINES

Another toxic influence occurs when parents coach from the sidelines. Most parents see no harm in coaching from the sidelines — nor do many coaches. But there is harm, albeit in quiet, subtle ways. One way is that it often creates *cognitive overload*. Cognitive overload refers to when a player, after hearing a parent coach from the sidelines, stops to think, and in stopping to think becomes unable to react to the ball and to the game situation with the speed and flexibility needed to succeed.

But the main reason for calling a parent coaching from the sidelines a toxic influence is that the players don't like it. Younger players rarely have the self-confidence to express their dislike of parents using words, but you can tell they don't like parents coaching from the sidelines by their worried expressions, confused looks, and other non-verbal indicators that they are no longer having fun. Therefore, manage this toxic influence. You can do so using the same methods you use to manage background anger, including pre-season meetings and respectful-tactful communications after games.

UMPIRES AND OPPOSING COACHES FAILING TO MEET THE NEEDS OF CHILDREN

If you coach youth baseball teams long enough, you are bound to come across an umpire or opposing coach who fails to meet the needs of a child, either by doing a poor job of assessing the needs or by ignoring them altogether. Here is an example of a well-meaning umpire doing a poor job of assessing the needs of a child player.

When Safety Wasn't the Issue

Mark was a good player who happened to wear glasses. From his seat on the bench, Mark's coach observed that the umpire was having a conversation with Mark in the batter's box. When it was clear Mark was becoming visibly upset, the coach went over to investigate. "Coach," the umpire said, "I can't let him bat with these glasses; it's unsafe." This assertion seemed highly illogical, but the coach thought it best to reason with the umpire. First, he sent Mark back to the on-deck circle so he would not be removed. Then, while trying to keep his composure, he protested, "Mark has been playing Little League for three years, and no one has ever asked him to remove his glasses. In my opinion, it would be more unsafe to allow him to hit without being able to see clearly. Plus, there is nothing in our league's rulebook that prohibits a player from batting with glasses on." The umpire, sensing that the coach was both composed and knowledgeable about the rules, relented and allowed Mark to hit.

We can assume that if Mark's coach had not acted forcefully and intelligently, the umpire's action would have been "toxic." At the very least, it would have ruined Mark's experience of playing that game.

With opposing coaches, failing to meet needs often happens when a coach is so focused on winning that winning trumps being sensitive to the needs of the children. In the concluding remarks, we will give an example of an opposing coach doing just that — failing to meet the needs of children because he was so wrapped up in winning. Here is an example of what we mean. In this later example as well as in the example given here of the umpire, we see the occasional need for a coach to protect his players from the poor judgment or poor behavior of umpires and opposing coaches. You need to prepare yourself to do the same.

Managing After the Games End

When managing the games of children, your job doesn't end with the end of the game. You will also need to see to it that players line up to respectfully shake hands with the players on the other team. And if the game was lost and was a particularly significant game for the players (that is, a playoff game), you will need to be available to help players manage their feelings around losing, as the following example illustrates.

After-game high fives are for cultivating good sportsmanship (photograph by Jay Reichheld).

A Card Trick After Losing a Game

Going into the playoffs, the Mets coach anticipated the possibility of his nine-year-olds having a difficult time if and when they lost a playoff game. He knew he had to do something to ensure that the season would end on a positive note. So, when the team did lose in the second round, he was prepared. As anticipated, his players took defeat hard, and many were crying as they walked off the field. But he was there to greet them with a baseball card for each player! With tear stains still on their cheeks, the players broke into smiles. Like so many nine-year-olds, the agony of defeat for these players was easily replaced with the happiness of trading baseball cards.

Sometimes too you will have to be there for individual players who blame themselves for a team's loss, as illustrated in the example on the following page.

There is lots to do following a game, lots to do to ensure that players go away with the right frame of mind.

When a Player Blames Himself for a Team's Loss

Jason was one of the least skilled players, a player who had a very difficult time fitting in, but being on the team for several years had helped. Most everyone had accepted him as a teammate. However, there were times when that acceptance was tested.

One such time was when he dropped a fly ball (a liner to right) that allowed the winning runs to score from second and third. After the game, Jason was very upset and blamed himself for letting down his teammates and losing the game. Some of his teammates did, in fact, blame him. Interestingly, the most skilled players did not blame Jason.

The coach pulled him aside and went to work on the way he was interpreting his role in the loss. He asked Jason if he threw the pitch that the hitter hit solidly for a line drive. He asked if he made the decision to not let Jason get pre-game outfield practice because he was needed to back up the coach hitting fungoes. He asked if Bobby, Sam, and Drew (the team's best players) were blaming him. After each question, Jason said, "No." Eventually he got the message—that any one error is apt to have several causes other than the play of the player making the error—and that the best, most confident players, the ones Jason could look up to, understood this and weren't into pointing fingers.

Conclusion

The main theme of this chapter has been about managing games with two goals in mind. One goal is to keep the team competitive so as to have a good chance of winning the game. Doing so is imperative if your players are to get the most enjoyment from the games.

However, in this chapter we also have been stressing that for child players, winning is apt to mean something different than it means to adults. For the players themselves, winning isn't everything. Therefore, throughout this chapter we have stressed the importance of managing the games of children with their agenda in mind, which is mostly about enjoying themselves and having a good experience playing the games. That is what it means to manage the games of children — to see to it that they enjoy themselves and have a good experience playing the games.

Part Three

Additional Essentials

In the final chapter and in the concluding remarks, we leave behind the issues featured in the previous two sections, the issues pertaining to teaching children how to play good baseball. In this last section, the focus is mostly on matters that go beyond baseball, such as helping children to develop good habits and character, establish a positive climate where children can feel good about being part of the group or team, and stimulate in children a love for the game in ways that go beyond simply playing the game. Here we attend to added essentials.

6

Character and Team Culture

There are players and teams with exceptional physical skills and the knowledge of how to hit, field, and pitch but who end up losing and deriving little satisfaction from playing baseball. The reasons have to do with failure to develop mental skills and the mind of an athlete. And there are players and teams who seriously undermine the satisfaction of playing baseball by the way they lose focus, fail to encourage others, misbehave, or treat others insensitively. These are issues having to do with character and team culture. Since they threaten to undermine the goal of children developing a love for baseball, we set aside an entire chapter to address them. In doing so, we address much more than problems having to do with playing baseball — for these are problems having to do with important life skills and habits of mind that lead to what is generally referred to as good character. This chapter deals with issues that go far beyond developing children as players. This chapter deals with issues having to do with developing children as people.

We divide this chapter into three parts. Each focuses on a separate issue related to character and team culture. In the first part, we focus on ways to help players develop goals, confidence, and those habits of mind needed in order to cope with anxiety and failure. In the second part, we focus on ways to manage problem behavior that promotes a positive team culture. In the third part, we focus on gender issues and how to create a positive culture on teams with both boys and girls.

Developing Positive Habits of Mind

Consider the following situation:

You're up. Bases loaded. Two outs. Last inning. Your team down by a run. A hit will drive in two runs and win the game. If you get out, it's all over. Everything is on the line ... it's up to you.

Now consider a similar situation:

You're pitching. Bases loaded. Two outs. Last inning. Your team is up by a run. Give up a hit, two runs score and it's all over. You get him out, and you win the game. Everything is on the line ... it's up to you.

Both of these situations are pressure situations in which young players are apt to fail not because they lack good mechanics, but because they don't know how to manage pressure and anxiety. When they become anxious, they begin to ask questions that make them even more anxious: *What if I mess up? What will my coach think? Are my parents watching? I can't do this! Everyone's counting on me! This kid is so much better than me!*

The increased anxiety leads to a variety of potential physical symptoms:

–Rapid breathing	–Stomachache or headache
–Inability to think straight	–Fatigue
–Quickened heart beat	–Tight muscles
–Sweaty palms or cold hands/feet	–Dizziness

Soon a player is unable to use his muscle memory and knowledge of mechanics to play good baseball.

To experience first-hand what we are talking about, try this experiment: Tell a young player to throw a ball at a target on the backstop, just for the fun of

Team spirit needs coaching too (photograph by Jay Reichheld).

it. Don't give him any further instructions; just instruct him to hit the target. Notice the carefree, relaxed manner in which he performs this activity. No pressure, no over-thinking necessary — no problem. Then ask him to hit that same target, but this time put something on the line. Offer him a sought-after prize for hitting it. Threaten him with extra running for missing it. While a select few may respond with better performance, the majority of young players will respond by replacing a relaxed manner with tension, worry, and fear. The activity will become stressful work. The fun will be gone. The target will seem harder to hit.

Most young players do not know what is required to mentally prepare for pressure situations; they haven't learned *how*. The common result: anxiety ➔ poor performance ➔ unhappiness ➔ anger ➔ frustration. It's no wonder 75 percent of athletes drop out of their sport by the time they are 13 years old. The game is no longer fun or exciting. The passion is no longer present in their baseball lives. In sum, all the physical gifts in the world will not help an athlete who is mentally unprepared.

What we are saying here is that it takes much more than physical skill for an athlete to become as good as he possibly can be. A baseball player with great hands, a strong bat, and a powerful arm will never reach his or her full potential without great concentration, motivation to play well, and ability to relax during important game situations. Here, then, we will continue the previous discussion (see Introduction) of *developing the mind of an athlete,* because a young player who is both physically *and* mentally skilled will play better and be more likely to develop a love for the game.

Few children learn how to motivate themselves, stay relaxed and focused, stay motivated and feel confident. That is why this section's discussion is important. Here, the discussion will be on describing ways you can help your players become self-motivated through setting goals, managing anxiety, and reacting positively to mistakes — all central to helping children develop the mind of an athlete.

Staying Focused, Relaxed, and Confident

"Focus on the field!" "Let's go, just relax!" "Be confident!" Wouldn't it be great if players could become focused, relaxed, and confident simply from hearing us give command instructions? If it were that easy, many more players would be top performers. Nobody would get nervous before or during a game. Everyone would have all the confidence in the world.

However, as we have already discussed, coaches and parents can turn blue in the face while shouting out command instructions, and a child who was having trouble relaxing before the shouting will probably have even greater trouble relaxing afterwards. Consider the situation of children working on a math assignment. If you were to shout something like "Come on, focus on the numbers! Just solve the equation!" to a nine-year-old who has little experience solving difficult multiplication problems, it probably won't help. In fact, it seems silly to assume that command instructions will miraculously create an arithmetical genius in a child with few math skills. The concept of relaxing the mind and body is just as foreign a concept to a child as is high-level multiplication, and so it is just as silly to expect command instructions to create Zen-like relaxation skills or what it takes to focus and feel confident.

Command instructions make players too self-conscious, and as mentioned in the Introduction, the smoothest, most flowing, most successful performances are those that *just happen,* without excessive thought attached to the action. When players are "mentally on," focused, and confident, chances are they are not thinking too much or being self-conscious.

But how to help players become mentally "on," focused, and confident is the question. To answer the question, we begin with an example that better defines the problem.

Pre-Game Anxiety

"Today's game against the Indians is HUGE," Brandon thinks as he nervously twiddles his thumbs in the car on the way to the ballpark. "Everyone's gonna be there—I have to play well." Later on, Brandon's anxiety heightens in the dugout while putting his cleats on. He quietly watches as excited teammates strut about, eagerly anticipating the start of the biggest game of the season.

During pre-game warm-ups, Brandon boots a few balls at his third base position. "What the heck's wrong with me?" he asks himself. "This never happens! What is going on today?" His harsh self-criticism becomes apparent to his teammates, who want nothing to do with his negative attitude before game time. Because of this, Brandon remains alone in the dugout, helplessly replaying his pre-game defensive mishaps in his mind.

The game starts, and Brandon is overcome with nerves. He feels jittery and confused, as if things are progressing in fast motion. "Please, don't hit the ball to me," he mutters to himself as he watches the leadoff hitter approach the batter's box. On the very first pitch, a hard ground ball is hit directly at Brandon. It goes right through his legs. The game is under way.

107

Brandon, like many of us, let his pre-game nerves get the best of him. But why? Shouldn't a few pre-game nerves help motivate and prepare a ballplayer for the game? Sometimes, yes. We all can benefit from low levels of anxiety. But *too much* anxiety can have detrimental effects, such as slower and more delayed reaction time and tighter, less fluid muscles. And so, it is important to understand the causes and effects of anxiety.

Actions do not simply happen by themselves. Rather, thoughts and feelings influence our actions. It makes sense then to help players cultivate those thoughts and feelings that help a player manage anxiety and prepare a player to succeed. Good pre-game thoughts and feelings are what collectively we refer to as confidence. For athletes, confidence is essential. With confidence, a player becomes more focused, more aware of his surroundings, and more in control. So, to stimulate good pre-game thoughts and feelings that ultimately build confidence, we begin with a discussion of using mental imagery.

USING MENTAL IMAGES

Confidence is not something innate. The saying "You either have it or you don't" doesn't apply to confidence. Rather, confidence is *built*. One great way to build confidence is by having players create *mental images* of what confidence looks like. Try these "imagery scripts" with players or come up with your own. Have players practice them before going to bed or during a quiet, uneventful period during the day — it should take only a few minutes. With practice, players will feel comfortable using them, at which point they can start incorporating them into their pre-game routine.

It is best to assume that your players have no prior knowledge of how to visualize success and confidence. You need to grab your players' attention immediately to get them interested in imagery. Ask them to recall a time before a game when they felt nervous and when they allowed their feeling nervous to affect their performance. Then explain how imagery can be used to combat choking from feeling nervous. Explain how famous and successful ballplayers have used and benefited from imagery!

To emphasize the way imagery works, take your players through an imagery test. Time your players individually as they sprint from home to first base. Then sit them down and ask them to imagine themselves as quick, springing cheetahs. To create speed, each player is to think of himself with powerful legs that spring forward with explosion and strength. Have them picture "fast energy" spreading through their feet, calves, upper legs, and arms.

Once your players have created the image of an explosive, energized, spring-

Imagery for Pitchers

• Before the game, picture yourself pitching against the team you will be facing. You are in control, pitching confidently to each batter. On the mound, you are hitting the catcher's glove with complete ease. You are able to change speeds and locations of your pitches with minimal effort. Take in all the senses. See your teammates, feel the relaxed energy, hear the crowd, smell the freshly cut grass. There's no anxiety. You know what to do, and it feels good doing it.

Imagery for Hitters

• Picture yourself up to bat in the actual game. You approach the plate with a clear plan, knowing just what you are looking for. You are facing a tough pitcher, but having a great at-bat. You see the ball clearly out of his hand and spoil his tough pitches. You wait for your pitch and then get it. You smash a line drive into the gap, exactly where you wanted it to go. Your hands and wrists are so quick that the ball flies off your bat with great speed. Take in all the senses of this great experience.

Imagery for Fielders

• Picture yourself making an error. Although you initially feel anxious, you are still extremely confident because your body feels loose and you are in control of yourself. See yourself fielding the next ground ball or fly ball that comes your way. You field it perfectly. You are having fun out there, and everything is coming so easily and naturally.

ing cheetah, have them again sprint from home to first base. In follow-up discussion you will find that your ballplayers will be stunned at how much quicker and faster they ran using the cheetah image. At this point it would be a good idea to explain exactly how imagery should be incorporated into their baseball lives (for example, starting with confidence imagery before games).

You can even use imagery to help players realize what they need to do to have a better team. An example is on the following page.

REFOCUSING AFTER A MISTAKE

All too often, the thoughts following mistakes are negative thoughts and questions such as *What will my coach and teammates think of me? My parents are going to be so disappointed! I'm the worst hitter on the team. I hate playing this posi-*

Imagery to Have a Better Team

Several games into the season, the head coach sensed that something was wrong. After continually witnessing members of his team screaming, yelling, and criticizing one another after each miscue, he figured something had to be done. At the end of a practice, he asked the team to imagine an ideal team. "What do players on the team look like? How do they act? What do they sound like? What are their superior characteristics?" The players on this less-than-ideal team were able to describe in impressive detail the appearance of an ideal youth baseball team—constant hustle, great communication, positive body posture, playing with enjoyment, always picking up teammates who struggle. The following game the players played exceptionally well together and won handily, 7–2.

---

tion. With such thoughts and questions, it is natural for a player to experience anxiety, frustration, and a lack of motivation to continue trying hard, all of which will make it more likely for another mistake to be made and for even more frustration to build—as illustrated in the following example.

When Errors Get the Best of a Player

Jason, one of the league's top defensive shortstops, confidently struts out to his position in the fourth inning. Known for his quick feet and rifle for an arm, Jason makes sure everyone in the stadium is watching as he shows off the goods during pre-inning warm-ups.

The first batter of the inning hits a routine two-hopper to Jason. While the entire team expects a sure out, they're stunned to find that Jason's throw to first sails over the first baseman's head and into the stands.

Nobody is more stunned than Jason. He can't help replaying the throw in his head, even during the next at-bat. "I can't believe I just made that stupid error," he cries to himself. "What are the other players going to think of me now?"

As Jason continues to worry, the current batter hits a sharp ground ball up the middle. Jason's wandering mind comes back to reality, but a second too late. He lunges for the ball as it scoots past him—it's a play Jason normally makes. Now there is nobody out and runners on the corners.

The single best thing to do in response to mistakes is to forget them and focus on the next play. Not an easy task for young players. They need your help. Here are suggestions for helping—things you can have players work on and do.

1. *Use a breath*—One of the easiest and most effective ways to reduce feelings of anxiety and refocus is to take a *good, deep* breath. Our breathing typically becomes quick and shallow when stressed. A good, deep breath allows oxygen to more efficiently enter the blood and the brain, which helps us think more clearly. When taking a deep breath, expand your stomach out as the air comes in. While breathing out, the air should flow out. Help players focus specifically on relaxing the muscles that are most tense. Help them scan their bodies, starting with the head, then the neck and shoulders, arms, hands, stomach, buttocks, legs, and feet. Finally, help them let their bodies relax and recharge with breaths.

2. *Use thoughts and self-statements*—Ask players what they typically say to themselves after a mistake or during a particularly important game situation. It's probably not positive or helpful. Becoming aware of negative self-statements is a first step to making changes in self-statements. Below are examples of how negative self-statements can be changed to positive ones.

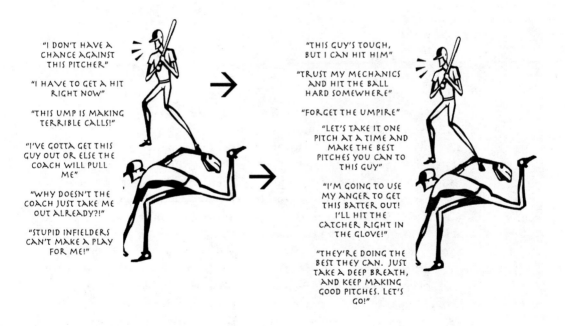

"I DON'T HAVE A CHANCE AGAINST THIS PITCHER"

"I HAVE TO GET A HIT RIGHT NOW"

"THIS UMP IS MAKING TERRIBLE CALLS!"

"I'VE GOTTA GET THIS GUY OUT OR ELSE THE COACH WILL PULL ME"

"WHY DOESN'T THE COACH JUST TAKE ME OUT ALREADY?!"

"STUPID INFIELDERS CAN'T MAKE A PLAY FOR ME!"

"THIS GUY'S TOUGH, BUT I CAN HIT HIM"

"TRUST MY MECHANICS AND HIT THE BALL HARD SOMEWHERE"

"FORGET THE UMPIRE"

"LET'S TAKE IT ONE PITCH AT A TIME AND MAKE THE BEST PITCHES YOU CAN TO THIS GUY"

"I'M GOING TO USE MY ANGER TO GET THIS BATTER OUT! I'LL HIT THE CATCHER RIGHT IN THE GLOVE!"

"THEY'RE DOING THE BEST THEY CAN. JUST TAKE A DEEP BREATH, AND KEEP MAKING GOOD PITCHES. LET'S GO!"

Start by incorporating positive self-talk into your practice routine. For example, help players immediately replace negative thoughts with positive ones after a poor batting practice.

3. *Use an object*—Another simple, useful way to refocus is to transfer negative energy onto an object. Here is what we mean: After making a poor play or otherwise doing something that causes tension, teach players to use a nearby object such as a cap, glove, or infield dirt to release tension and allow players to relax. Some players find it helpful after making a fielding error to punch the pocket of their glove as hard as possible, so as to *crush* the error and start fresh! Other players find it useful to remove the glove from their hand as a way to refocus and "remove" all negative thoughts and feelings associated with the error. In response to aswing-and-a-miss, a batter can step out of the box, take a deep breath, and squeeze all of his anger into his bat to use as power for the next pitch, transferring what could be perceived as helpless frustration into localized power.

Once a player has allowed himself to relax and eliminate negative thoughts, the player should focus on hitting, pitching, or fielding; that is, he should focus on playing the game.

Allocating several minutes each day to practicing these and other ways to relax and refocus will make players stronger and better prepared for anything that may occur during the game. Young players must understand that mental skills, as with physical skills, must be practiced and honed before any real change occurs. Here's an example.

Practicing Ways to Get Back on Track

Timmy would break into tears when confronted with stress—a fielding error, a strikeout, even a raised voice from a teammate. After a particularly emotional game, the coach approached Timmy and asked, "Is that a helpful response to making a mistake? In other words, does getting upset and frustrated allow you to do better during your next at-bat or your next groundball?" When Timmy said no, the coach replied, "Then what is the perfect response to get yourself back on track? What will help you play your BEST?" Timmy and his coach then devised a plan, a response to stress. Timmy would take two deep breaths, wipe the frustration away with a soft pound of the glove or a squeeze of the bat, come up with one positive thought about the previous play, and then focus attention on the present. With a few days of practice, Timmy felt confident enough to use his routine during his next game. After an early-inning strikeout, Timmy bounced back and followed with a great at-bat his next time up.

Goal-Setting and Motivation to Succeed

Goal-setting is another way to help players develop the mind of an athlete as well as develop overall good mental habits. Goal-setting is especially important for getting players to become self-motivated. Start getting players to set goals by posing these questions to them: *Coming into every season, every game, every inning, every pitch, do you know exactly what you want to accomplish? Do you have a plan for each situation in the field, on the mound, or in the box? Do you set goals?*

Most young players will answer "no" to these questions. Furthermore, most will have never set goals, not once — even players who have been successful and who are physically gifted. The problem with this is that without setting goals, players are apt to have only limited motivation or drive to succeed.

Sometimes ballplayers respond, "Sure, I set goals. In fact, before the season I set a goal to win the league championship, to be the best pitcher on my team, or to lead my team in hitting." Well, that's great! Setting goals is the first step. However, making sure that goals are set in such a way that they can be achieved is the next step.

Players will find that setting goals for themselves and putting goals down on paper will help motivate them and make them work harder. Whatever the goal, it should be *personally important* to the player. Regardless of its importance to a teammate or coach, it should matter to *that player*. A child should be invested in whatever he sets out to do. Below are guidelines that will help children set goals as best they can.

GOALS SHOULD BE SPECIFIC

Clearly indicate what you want to accomplish, both for the season (long-term goals) and even for each game or practice (short-term goals).

- *"I want to do well"* is not specific at all.
- *"I want to become a better fielder"* is more specific.
- *"I want to get to balls more quickly"* is wonderfully specific.

Be specific in measurable terms. Athletes will be more likely to *want* to accomplish a goal if there are numbers or measurements involved and if there is a **target date attached to the goal.**

- *"I want to hit better"* is not measurable since it is not clear what hitting better means here.

- *"I want to swing only at strikes"* is more measurable, though there is no baseline measure or timetable mentioned here.

- *"I want to reduce my swinging at balls that are clearly outside the strike zone to zero, starting now"* is perfectly measurable AND time-sensitive.

GOALS SHOULD BE CONTROLLABLE

The goal "to win today" is not one a player has control over since winning depends so much on the performance of opponents and teammates. All a player can control is HIMSELF. Here is a table to illustrate the distinction between goals where a player has control versus those where a player does not:

Can Control	*Can't Control*
YOUR attitudes	Umpires
YOUR reactions & responses	Weather
YOUR preparation & performance	Equipment
YOU	Teammates' reactions, attitudes, beliefs, actions
	Coaches' reactions, attitudes, beliefs, actions
	Fans
	Other people
	Outcome of the game

Goals should be tied to practicing and not just to performing during games. *"Correct my swing path by taking 50 extra swings a day so that I hit more line drives"* is a perfect example of a goal that is within a player's control and tied to practice.

In addition to encouraging individual goal-setting, set up a *team goal-setting program* as well. Together with your players and before the start of the season, come up with two or three realistic and challenging goals for the season and indicate *how they will they be attained.* What will it take to win the championship? How will you become the best fielding team in the league? Monitor, evaluate, and adjust goals as needed. Making a goal board can be helpful in uniting players to achieve common goals as well as providing a written document that can be shown to the team throughout the season. Once you and your players have established team goals, ask your players to come up with individual goals. Meet with each player briefly and consider meaningful questions such as

- What do you want to accomplish this season?
- What will be better or different about you by the end of the season?

Put players' goals in writing, and offer regular feedback on how they are doing. The goal-setting sheet on the following page can act as an effective, simple handout that young athletes can easily complete.

Players will be more motivated to play harder if practice goals are made in addition to goals for the season. Below are some examples of practice goals that players can set with the guidance of the coach:

- *"Take 20 extra swings and practice hitting the ball the other way."* For each successful opposite field line drive during batting practice, offer them a *home run ball*, in which their aim is to hit it as long and as far as possible. Make it creative. Stir up some excitement.
- *"Become the best, most supportive teammate possible by offering encouragement and support to teammates throughout practice."* Come up with team slogans and mottos that can be used to relax an anxious player, energize a fatigued player, or support a teammate after a bad play. Ask team members to describe what a perfectly supportive team looks like, acts like, sounds like, etc. Have them emulate these characteristics all year.
- *"Have more fun during practice by SMILING 35 extra times during the course of practice."* This may sound awkward and initially uncomfortable, but it will certainly loosen up the players and add an element of humor to the sometimes-humorless practice schedule.

In sum, setting specific, controllable goals will motivate athletes to try harder, focus more clearly, and gain a sense of direction and meaning for playing baseball.

Managing Problem Behavior

When players fool around on the bench, space out in the outfield, and act in unsupportive ways to teammates, we lump these and other negative behaviors together as "problem" behaviors. Furthermore, our natural inclination is to manage these behaviors by reacting after they happen rather than trying to prevent them from happening in the first place. And in reacting to these behaviors, our natural inclination is to manage them by telling players what they must stop doing ("Stop talking," "Stop fooling around," etc.).

Telling players to stop misbehaving or stop behaving in unhelpful ways is necessary at times, but there is much more to managing problem behavior effec-

Name: _____

Baseball Goal Setting

Congratulations on setting goals for yourself! You'll find that setting goals and actually *writing them down on paper* will help motivate you and make you work harder at achieving them! Remember, each goal should be specific and important to you in your life. Let's set some goals together that you would like to accomplish this season!

Player's Goals

Date: _____

Goal #1: _____

_____

How will you achieve this goal? What do you have to do in order to accomplish it?

a. _____

b. _____

c. _____

d. _____

Notes: _____

_____

_____

_____

Target date: _____

tively and positively so as to support the players' development and the development of a positive team culture. That is our aim here — to give you a broader, more effective and more positive approach to managing problem behavior so that you develop a positive team culture.

There are a number of things to consider when managing problem behavior. First, what adults call problem behavior is often what children do naturally. For example, to fool around on the bench or lose focus in the outfield aren't signs of character flaws; they are signs of children being children. Keeping this in mind should allow for a more positive approach to behavior management, one that includes being firm when needed but not one that includes being harsh because we think children should know better.

Second, much that is labeled misbehavior or inappropriate behavior is actually behavior reflecting what children have yet to learn. Experienced, professional teachers know this, so they teach children things that non-professionals don't even know need to be taught, such as how to sit and how to speak to someone in respectful ways.

In the case of baseball, you can assume that many of your players simply don't know how to encourage a teammate who has made an error or how to react to a teammate who has just hit a home run or even how to take the field and hustle after an inning is over. You need to teach them with verbal explanations and demonstrations. For example, don't just explain what it means to hustle out to the outfield after an inning is over; during practice sessions, hustle out yourself to show them. In sum, the guideline here is to treat problem behaviors with the assumption that your players have yet to learn and then figure out how to teach players not only with verbal explanations but also with demonstrations.

Teaching players can mean individual instruction as well as instruction during team meetings. In team meetings, teach players how to behave when they think an umpire has made a mistake. Teach them how to behave on the bench. Teach them how to be good winners and good losers. In other words, don't assume they know these things. Teach them. Doing so will help players in ways that go beyond playing baseball, since lots of what you teach applies to life in general.

Third, prevent problem behavior from occurring in the first place. We've seen this several times before, such as when we suggested assigning an infielder the job of calling out situations ("One out, player on first!" or "Two outs, player on first and third," etc.) to prevent outfielders from completely losing their focus. Similarly, organize practice sessions so players are always occupied by making use of stations and your own monitoring. Unoccupied and unmonitored children usually mean children fooling around.

Fourth, after problem behavior occurs, lead with something positive before correcting players. Problems are to some extent in the eye of the beholder; that is, in the way they are defined. We may define a child losing focus in the outfield as a problem, but from a different perspective it's possible to see the child as being curious and interested in bugs in the grass. The point here is that any problematic situation can be *reframed* so that it is no longer a problem.

There is usually something positive to say about any situation, so find and lead with that approach. Doing so will open a child up to listening to your suggesting changes. So, for example, if a child has hit a single and then races to second without first noting that a teammate has stopped at second base, don't lead with the comment that he should have been more aware. First, compliment him for being aggressive on the base paths, and then help him learn to combine being aggressive with making good "reads." This is what we mean by reframing and always leading with something positive.

Almost any problem situation can use reframing. Fooling around on the bench can become "You guys know how to have fun." Getting mad at a teammate who has just made an error can become "The game really means a lot to you." The point here is that there is something positive even in situations where initially there seems to be only negatives — and it is your job to figure this out. You'll find that when you make reframing your habitual response, players will be much more responsive to you in turn and much more likely to continue to develop a love for the game.

Finally and most important, cultivate positive relationships with all of your players, especially with those players where behavior management is an issue. Remember, when players come to value their relationship with you, they are more likely to listen to you and want to behave themselves. The reverse is also true. When players sense you disapprove of them, don't like them, or otherwise have a negative view of them, they are less likely to listen and more likely to misbehave. So before misbehavior occurs, show each player your positive attention and give each player your positive support and encouragement — it will pay dividends if and when the time comes when you must manage problem behavior.

In sum, there are positive ways to manage problem behavior. Use them. The table on the following page summarizes what has been suggested.

Coaching Teams with Both Boys and Girls

We have come a long way with respect to treating girls fairly in sports. Thirty years ago, mixed teams with both boys and girls were rare. Now, they are fast

Things to Consider When Managing Problem Behavior

1. Problem behavior is natural to children, so don't treat the problem behaviors of children as character flaws.

2. Many problem behaviors are reflections of what children have yet to learn, so teach them.

3. Prevent problem behaviors from occurring in the first place (e.g., organizing practice sessions so that everyone is always active and involved).

4. After a problem behavior occurs, lead with something positive to say.

5. Cultivate positive relationships with all players.

On youth baseball teams, girls and boys should simply be players (photograph by Jay Reichheld).

becoming the norm. Nevertheless, girls still are sometimes treated differently and in ways that undermine the quality of their experience. Here, we need to say a few words about managing teams made up of both boys and girls. The message is simple: In youth baseball, all children should be treated as *players*.

This means a player's gender should not change the way you teach mechanics, manage practices, manage games, and, in general, coach baseball. We say this for good reasons. First, before puberty, girls are not physically less capable of playing baseball. If anything, they are stronger than boys — at least stronger with respect to bone structure (Wiggins, 1996). Girls, then, have just as much potential to be good youth baseball players as do boys. Second, on average, girls want to compete and develop skills just as much as boys do. Third, girls and boys are better off respecting each other as players than they are when we encourage misguided stereotyping. So check your own assumptions when coaching girls and insist always that when playing youth baseball, gender is irrelevant.

Here are a few examples to indicate the problems you should avoid or be able to handle. The following example illustrates what can happen when a coach assumes a girl is likely to be a less skilled player.

Assuming Girls Can't Play

During the Royals' practice, Coach Johnson divided his players into two groups, sending the first group to field ground balls and the second group to practice fly balls. After half an hour of practice, the groups switched places. However, Coach Johnson told Maria to remain in the outfield when the groups switched. Maria was bored by always playing in the outfield. She wanted to practice fielding ground balls and demonstrate her skills so she could have a chance to play infield during the game. Maria worked up the courage to ask Coach Johnson for infield practice, but she was refused. It was not long after that Maria started missing practices and games, and at the end of the season, she had played the last game of her career.

The first example on the following page illustrates another damaging assumption, namely, that girls should get a softer kind of coaching or no coaching at all.

Finally, the second example illustrates that it is the coach's responsibility to teach the boys on the team that girls are no different from them with respect to their being players.

Soft Coaching for Girls

Players for the Pirates were fielding ground balls during practice on a field that was rough and pocketed with divots. Kimberly was first in line to field a ground ball. She ran onto the field, got into the ready position and waited for Coach McIntyre to hit the ball. Kimberly waited for the slow grounder to reach her, but just before the ball got to her glove, it hit a divot and hopped to the right of her body. She extended her glove side arm, but the ball had already passed her. Kim retrieved the ball and returned to the end of the line. The next few players fielded the balls without error and without interference from divots. Then Billy missed a ground ball because of a bad hop off of a divot. Coach McIntyre walked to shortstop and demonstrated how to charge and round the ball as it comes off the bat. "Get to the ball before it can take a bad hop," Coach McIntyre advised. While waiting for his next turn, Billy practiced the footwork of rounding the ball. During his next turn he came through the ball and scooped it up before it reached the divot. Coach McIntyre yelled, "Excellent work, Billy. I knew you could do it."

Teaching Boys How to Respect Girls

The White Sox knew that the Mayfair Cleaners had a girl pitcher who could throw a mean fastball. Yet they were surprised when she came into pitch as a reliever in the fifth inning with the bases loaded and one out. Brian, a power hitter for the White Sox, stepped to the plate with a chance to bring in the tying run from third base, but he struck out. When Brian walked into the dugout a teammate teased, "You got struck out by a girl." Brian did not respond to the teammate, but remained sullen and upset. Jake came to the plate next and grounded out. The White Sox players took the field slower than usual. Their enthusiasm had been knocked out of them, and Anna finished the game without allowing a run. Anna continued to dominate the league that season. When the Mayfair Cleaners played the Expos, the players and some of the parents for the Expos expressed shock that a girl defeated them. One player asked, "Is she really a girl?" Before the teams shook hands, the Expos coach called his players into a huddle, and while showing them a baseball, said, "The baseball doesn't care whether it is being thrown by a boy or girl, so why should you? When a pitcher is pitching to you, that pitcher is a pitcher and you are a batter. There are no girls versus boys in baseball." As the Expos and Mayfair Cleaners shook hands, two Expos players said to Anna, "Hey, you did a great job!"

In sum, your approach to coaching girls should be simple. Girls should be coached the same way you coach boys — as *youth players*.

Conclusion

As this chapter shows, playing baseball is more than about mechanics. It is also about showing character and ability to manage anxiety, build confidence, and refocus after making mistakes. It is also about being a good teammate and showing respect for others. All this is heady stuff, but with good coaching, it is not too heady for even young players.

Conclusion: Children and the Game of Baseball

Baseball has a special place among the sports played in America. For over a century, baseball has been our country's "national pastime." And while other sports make legitimate claims that they are number one in popularity, no sport has had the same impact on our culture as has baseball. There is something quintessentially American about baseball. It is a team sport, but it is also a sport that features individuals. It is a sport calling for sacrifice and self-discipline, but it is also a sport where one can relax and have fun. There is energy in baseball, but there is also something lazy too — as in lazy by the pool on a hot summer's day.

Most of all, there are relationships in baseball that can matter a great deal: father-son relationships to be sure (see this book's foreword for an example) but also relationships between parents and daughters, between coaches and players, and, of course, between the players themselves who sometimes become lifelong friends.

Perhaps no other American sport has been so successful at supporting lifelong relationships as has baseball. We think the reasons are several. First, involvement with baseball begins not only on the "diamond" but whenever a toddler is encouraged to throw the ball. It begins very early on, at home with a parent and child playing catch and throw. Later, it progresses to playing in more elaborate ways, with friends and rules. Later still, it is fed by the games played by professionals, by trading cards, by reading newspapers to get the "box scores" and numerous activities other than actually playing the game.

That is what makes baseball so enduring. Even when not playing the game or watching others play the game, it is possible to be deeply involved with baseball. And when that involvement happens, something good occurs, something without much that is negative, and something that connotes values we can all ascribe to.

Because baseball has been so good to us, we have a special responsibility when passing it along to the next generation. As this book has tried to show, that

Youth baseball should be about being with friends (photograph by Jay Reichheld).

responsibility has nothing to do with using baseball to make children into great athletes or to get scholarships for college. Nor does it have to do with winning championships.

Unfortunately, there are plenty of coaches and parents who don't see matters this way — or at least, don't act as if they do. There are plenty whose actions indicate that the value of winning trumps the value of children having a positive experience playing baseball. Often, those actions are rationalized as being good for children or good because they teach children to play by the rules. But they aren't good for children if they get in the way of children loving the game. On the following page is an example of a coach who probably rationalized his maneuver to rattle the other team's pitcher by saying something like "We all need to play by the rules."

We are responsible, then, for seeing to it that children play *their* game, not ours, so that they come to experience the simple joys we once experienced of playing a game they have come to love.

Trying to Rattle a Child with a Technicality

It was the first round of the playoffs, and tensions were high. Right after the first pitch of the game, the opposing coach protested that the pitcher, Chris, was breaking contact with the rubber during the course of his windup. The protest was obviously the coach's calculated attempt to "rattle" the young pitcher and use a technicality to increase his team's chances of winning.

Chris' coach called time-out, walked to the mound, and said to Chris, "Don't worry about anything. I'm going to talk to the umpire, but don't let the other team use these dirty tricks to break your focus." Then, keeping his best composure, the coach argued his case to the umpire—that his counterpart was seeking to unnerve his young pitcher on a technicality that not even major league umpires uphold, and that the toe-tapping had no effect on the actual pitch. The umpire listened and then agreed. Chris returned to pitching without having to change his motion.

Throughout this book, we have tried to show that the simple joys include knowing how to play this not-so-simple game. However, in doing so, we have also tried to show that it is not in becoming great baseball players that children experience joy and a love for the game. It is in their participating in the games themselves and in their developing enough skills to have those occasional moments of glory—a double to right-center field or a leaping catch to end a game—moments that can last a lifetime in memory.

In the final analysis, we owe our children memories—great memories of playing baseball, the kinds of memories that mark a love for the game, and the kinds that make us feel good about being alive. There is a spirit in baseball that comes not from our coaching to win but from everyone participating who loves the game. If the day ever comes when children fail to develop a love for the game, that spirit will be gone and we'll have no one to blame but ourselves. We hope that day never comes and that all of us will become much better at helping children love the game.

Part Four
Appendices

There are hundreds of drills and games to choose from and almost as many good resources. Deciding which drills and games are best depends on who your players are and how far along they are in their development as players. However, there are a few drills and games that are widely used and appropriate for a variety of age groups, so we will mention only these few in the appendices and encourage you to consider the rest, adding your own invented drills and games to suit your players' needs.

As for resources, there are also many in the form of books, films, and websites, so many that only a sampling are included here. The sampling gives some indication of what is available. Consider the sampling, but also consider exploring on your own.

Appendix One: Drills

Drills for Hitting and Baserunning

HITTING OFF A TEE / TEE ON PLATE

This is an excellent drill for checking for proper stance and for helping young players swing down and through the ball, which will result in their concentrating on hitting the ball up the middle. Furthermore, because the tee can be placed at different heights, it provides a way for players to learn how to hit balls in different locations.

The key here is to provide enough supervision so that players can learn to evaluate and correct their mistakes on their own, including mistakes related to improper grip or stance. Players should see that there is a direct connection between their topping the ball or popping the ball up and their having an improper grip, stance or improper swing.

HITTING OFF A TEE
PLACED WELL IN FRONT

This drill helps players keep their hands going through the middle of the hitting zone rather than lunging and trying to pull the ball. The task for players is to drive the ball up the middle (see Chapter Four for further discussion and photo illustration).

HIGH-TEE DRILL

The high-tee drill is essential for ensuring a proper, fundamentally sound swing. Set the tee up to where the top is level with the player's chest, and have him swing as if it were a regular tee. The high-tee is a great drill for fixing many problems that plague young hitters, such as dropping the back shoulder and not swinging on a level plane. With the high tee, it forces the hitter to swing directly to the ball in order to hit it properly.

ADDITIONAL TEE DRILLS

- Top-Hand Drill: Have players use only the top hand to take the bat right to the ball.
- Power Hand Drill: Have players use only the bottom hand to develop hand strength.
- Multiple Location Drill: Place the tee at one of three locations — inside, away, and middle. Have players work on hitting the ball to the pull side, the opposite field, and up the middle, respectively.

SOFT TOSS

Much like the tee, soft toss is designed to practice the correct swing and diagnose flaws. The player should assume his normal stance, with his shoulder towards a fence or net.

The coach or partner should toss the ball (either hardball, tennis ball, or rag ball), not quickly but without an arc, about six inches off the back hip of the player The player should then take a normal swing and make contact with the ball in the hitting zone, hopefully hitting a line drive. Similar to using the tee, the ball position of the toss can be altered, simulating different pitch types. This drill is especially effective in helping players who have a tendency to "drift forward" or not keep their weight or hands back during the swing.

TRACKING PITCHED TENNIS BALLS WITH DIFFERENT COLORED DOTS

To get players to carefully watch pitched balls from the moment a ball leaves a pitcher's hand to the moment the ball connects with the bat, throw tennis balls with different colored dots, and have players yell out the color of the dot as the ball crosses the plate. You can make this into a game and have correct calls serve as hits and incorrect calls serve as outs.

DUCK AND COVER

Have players practice the proper way to avoid getting hit by a pitch. A coach should pitch rag or tennis balls directly at players, who should turn their front shoulder toward the catcher while bending slightly at the waist.

TAPE BALLS

Fashion tape balls by balling up pieces of masking tape into a ball no bigger than a golf ball. Pitch them to batters much like a normal pitch. The small size of the ball forces hitters to keep their eyes on the ball and stay focused through the entire swing. Batters can use either a regular bat, or if they are advanced enough, a broomstick.

PING-PONG PADDLE

This drill is designed to work on extending the top hand through the swing. The paddle is held in the left hand, and the same procedure as soft toss is used. However, instead of baseballs, ping-pong balls or other small objects are used to make contact. This drill not only improves hand-eye coordination; it also reinforces the need to extend the top hand down and through the swing, therefore eliminating the common tendency to "drop" the hands and swing in an incorrect arc path.

BALANCE BEAM

This drill is designed to improve players balance and in so doing correct a number of swing flaws. Coaches should obtain a number of two-by-four pieces of wood, long enough to accommodate a typical stride length. Have players take their normal stances and attempt to hit the ball off a tee into a fence, all the while standing on the two-by-four. Ideally, players should be able to take their normal stride and swing without falling off the wood. This drill can also prevent stepping in the bucket, as players need to step straight to the pitcher in order to maintain balance atop the wood.

FOUR-CORNER BUNTING

Split your team up into four groups and station each group at a separate base. Designate each base for a different kind of bunting (sacrifice, bunt for a base hit, squeeze, and choice) and have your players throw to each other as you walk around and monitor their progress.

THROUGH DRILL

This drill is ideal for helping hitters run through first base, as opposed to slowing up just before reaching the bag. Oftentimes, young runners will slow down when approaching a base, causing the throw to beat them. Have all your players line up behind home plate, and put the first player into the batter's box, as if he is hitting. On "go," the batter should take a swing, simulating a live game, and run towards first. At first base, you should instruct your players by yelling either "Two two two," signaling for them to run to second, or "Bag bag bag," signaling for them to overrun first base and then slow up.

DOWN DRILL

This drill helps players learn to listen when they are on the base paths. Have the players line up at first base and on your "go" have them run to third base. At third base, you should instruct players to either "get down," "slow up," or "go go go," indicating that they should slide, go in standing up, or make a turn and run home, respectively.

"OLYMPICS"

This drill is designed to teach players to "cut the bases" properly. Coaches should pair up players of similar foot speed. One player starts at second base, and the other at home plate. They simply race, seeing who can be the first to advance two bases. The player at second runs only to home, and the player who starts at home runs only to second. Whoever reaches their respective destination first is the winner. During this drill, impress upon players the need not only to be fast, but more importantly to cut the bases properly, sharpening the angle by taking a "banana path." Again, this drill can be team-based by dividing players into two teams who compete to see who wins the most races.

TIME TRIALS

This drill is simple, but not necessarily productive or enjoyable for slower runners. Use a stopwatch or some other accurate timepiece, and time individual players running all the way around the bases. Coaches can also time players from home to first, or any permutations of running around the bases. Players will get competitive about this, but it can be an effective way to break up a long practice.

RUNNING THROUGH FIRST BASE

For efficiency, set up two or three parallel first base lines next to one another, and at your signal, have players go from their batting stance into their sprint to first base — encouraging players to run through first base and then turn slightly to the right and assume the athlete's position. This drill can also serve as a speed competition.

Drills for Fielding

LONG TOSS

Long toss is when two players start throwing to one another at a typical distance (20 to 30 feet apart) and then keep backing up after each couple of throws, until the players are throwing and catching at a long distance. Despite the distance, they are still trying to throw and catch using proper mechanics and keeping the ball on a line. This drill is useful for warming up before games, especially for pitchers, so it should be carried out without overthrowing and while being careful not to injure the arm. Furthermore, the drill gets children's interest, because increasing the distance presents a graded challenge. You can make this drill into a game by having players start over (from the beginning distance) whenever they drop the ball or throw off line. However, for most of the time, it is best to use this drill simply as a warm-up.

RAPID FIRE

This drill involves playing catch at a usual distance but at a rapid fire speed. It is often played as a competition, either between pairs of players or against the clock. Players can measure their progress against other pairs, the clock, or both.

FOUR CORNERS

This is another warm-up drill, especially suited for warming up before real games. It consists of having a player at each base (including home plate) and whipping the ball around the diamond clockwise first (to practice their pivot) and then counter-clockwise. To insert a game-like atmosphere, the drill can be used with a stopwatch.

TENNIS/RAG BALL FOR OUTFIELD FLIES

To reduce the fear factor and to encourage children to sprint to fly balls and catch them with the glove between the ball and nose, use tennis or rag balls in drills for catching fly balls — at least until players develop enough ability to catch real baseballs correctly and without fear. Also, start outfield drills by throwing to players, and then progress to hitting fly balls. Throw after players assume a ready position (throwing to both sides, front and back; that is, throwing in all directions), and then throw after they start running in a particular direction (throwing in front of players to emphasize their needing to sprint to the ball as if they don't have a glove on).

QUARTERBACK DRILL

The outfielder starts the drill to the side of the coach. On "go," the outfielder sprints in a "route" pattern similar to a football receiver. You, as the coach, throw the baseball, which the outfielder must track down and catch.

PICK-UP AND THROW

This is a nice drill to help players get the feel for receiving ground balls and then throwing using a proper grip. The drill starts with a player placing the ball on the ground in front of him. Then, either on your command or on his own, the player picks up the ball and throws to a target. The emphasis should be on completing the pick-up and throwing smoothly, quickly, and with the proper C-grip.

TWO LINE UNDERHAND ROLLS

In this drill, players form two lines, and you roll (underhand) balls to the head of each line. While one player tosses a ball back, you roll another ball to the player at the head of the other line so as to keep everything moving at a quick pace. This is a safe and simple way to have players practice fielding ground balls with their backsides down and their feet and glove out in front, forming a triangle.

FOUR-ON-ONE PEPPER

You or a player can hit soft ground balls to four players lined up in a row and only a few yards away — doing so fairly rapidly. This drill helps with the eye-hand coordination involved in fielding ground balls. After receiving a ball, players roll the ball back to you while you are in the process of hitting to the next player.

SHORT-HOP PAIRS

In this drill, players pair up and throw (not hard) at each other's feet so that each player practices short-hopping.

TEXAS LEAGUERS

Place your players in their respective positions and either hit or throw pop flies in between the outfielders and the infielders. Known as "Texas Leaguers," this drill fosters communication between fielders and develops fly ball fielding skills. Remember, the shortstop has the authority to direct who fields a ball over other infielders, outfielders have authority over the infield, and the center fielder has authority over other outfielders.

RUN-DOWN DRILL

Place two infielders in line about 50–60 feet apart and have a runner, with batting helmet on, next to one of the infielders. On your signal, the runner should begin running, trailed by the first infielder who has the ball. The goal of the runner should be to not get thrown out in fewer than three throws, while the goal of the infielders should be to tag the runner in no more than two throws.

CROSS-OVER DRILL

In order to double the number of ground balls fielded in a given drill, have two coaches hit fungoes to the infielders. Each infield position should have two or three players working in rotation. The coach on the first base line hits to third and short; the coach on the third base line hits to first and second.

GLOVE WORK

Roll a ball to the fielder who is approximately 10 feet away in the crouched stance with an open glove. Don't throw the ball too far from the fielder; the purpose of this drill is to encourage glove work, not footwork. Vary between hard and soft ground balls to the fielder's slight left and slight right. Remind fielders to keep their gloves in front of their body and to adopt the "alligator" position when receiving the ball with two hands. With glove work repetition, the fielder will learn to watch the ball into the glove and improve.

Short Hops

This drill can follow glove work, as it requires the same equipment and positioning. The fielder, who has maintained the crouched, open-gloved, on-the-balls-of-the-feet stance, scoops and picks short hops created by a teammate kneeling several feet away. The kneeling teammate should keep the fielder "on his toes" by mixing in soft and hard short hops, as well as throwing directly at the fielder or to the fielder's left or right. Fielders should assume the "alligator" position, with the upper hand keeping the ball from coming out of the glove. This drill promotes adeptness with the glove and the feet. Short hops can be done on a dirt or grass playing surface.

Tags

In this drill, use one of the actual bases or an imaginary base. Teach your infielders the skill of slapping a tag on a base. Use actual runners if you want to make the drill more realistic. Encourage your runners to slide on, behind, in front, to the left, and to the right of the base. Teach fielders to bring the glove down (actually slap the glove down) to the front part of the base as quickly as possible to meet the runner. Perform this drill rapidly; in other words, have several fielders at each position so that once one fielder has successfully tagged a base, the next one can step up.

Drop to a Knee

This is a good drill for outfielders working on keeping a harder hit ground ball in front of them. Spread half of your outfielders in a long line in the outfield, and the other half a fair distance away with a ball. Pair each fielding outfielder receiving a ball with another outfielder, who is holding a ball. Once the receiving fielders have assumed the pre-pitch, crouched, and aggressive position, the ball-carrying outfielders should throw a hard ground ball toward their partner. The ball should not be too far out of the partner's reach, but should be thrown hard enough so that it requires the partner to field the ball down on a knee. Dropping to a knee and keeping the glove in front of the body will ensure that the ball stays in front. Once the first group of outfielders successfully field 10 hard-hit ground balls on a knee, have the pairings switch places.

ONE-KNEE DRILLS

Often when young players throw, they short-arm the throw; that is, they fail to utilize the "lead arm" and fail to follow through. One-knee drills help remedy these problems. Players should drop to their dominant knee (righties to their right knee, lefties to their left knee), close their shoulder, and face their partner. In this position, players will have an easier time following the coach's commands because only their upper body is isolated. Young players working on overcoming throwing problems won't have to worry about footwork. They can focus on arm path.

Touch the Wall

To prevent *short-arming,* players will remain on their knee and start with their throwing arm on the ground with a ball. Once you yell out, "Touch the wall!" players will bring their arm from this neutral position past their hip and up to the sky. Their throwing arm should not be fully extended, but rather slightly bent at the elbow, which is raised to about shoulder height. The ball should be facing away from their body as if they are touching an imaginary wall behind them.

Lead Arm

To reinforce lead arm action while throwing, players will remain on their knee and once again start with their throwing arm on the ground with a ball in their hand. Once you yell out "Lead arm!" players will bring their lead arm (left arm for righties, right arm for lefties) to about shoulder height so that the elbow points directly to the partner. Make sure each player's front shoulder remains closed until the ball is released.

Follow Through

To reinforce following through after a throw, players will remain on their knee and start with their throwing arm touching an imaginary wall. From this position each player will throw the ball to his or her partner and focus on following through. That is, once the ball is released, the player's chest should end up over his front knee. This will give you a sense of whether the player is shifting his weight when he throws (in which case the follow-through will naturally occur)

136

or if the player is short-arming the ball or perhaps even slowing his throwing motion down before the ball is released. See Chapter Four for further discussion and a photo illustration.

STRIDE WHEN THROWING

This is a good drill for players who misplant their stride foot when throwing; that is, those who incorrectly step with their stride foot (left foot for righties, right foot for lefties) when throwing the ball. For this drill, have each player partner up and break the drill into several parts by calling out certain commands. The command "Stride!" should prompt fielders to point their stride foot directly at the target. Young players who often make poor throws have a tendency to keep their stride foot too closed or too open, or they simply do not stride at all. Make sure that upon the "Stride!" command, fielders take a small step forward, pointing the toes of the stride foot directly at the target. Not until you say "Throw!" should fielders release the ball and finish with a proper follow-through.

TWO HANDS

Another common mistake made by young fielders is the failure to catch the ball with two hands. Dedicate a few minutes at the beginning of practice to focusing on using two hands to catch the ball. This can be incorporated into "Stride!" While one fielder is working on properly planting the stride foot, the other can be working on receiving the ball with the glove and using the throwing hand as a means of securing the ball in the glove.

QUICK HANDS

Quick hands can be done with a normal infielder's glove or with a paddle/flat glove. Even a makeshift cardboard box glove will do. Many times during a game, infielders need to get the ball out of their glove quickly in order to make an out. Quick hands are needed. In this drill, two fielders stand about 20 feet apart and toss a ball to each other, working on making a quick transfer from glove (or paddle) to throwing hand. Fielders should each try to make and receive 20 "quick hands" throws before stopping. If a player drops the ball during the transfer, start again from zero and work up to 20. Quick hands should be done at a relatively fast pace. The more practice with this drill, the quicker and more comfortable the fielder will be during in-game situations.

FOUR-WAY INFIELD GROUNDERS

This drill offers ground ball practice to each of the four infield positions simultaneously. Four people, preferably coaches who can hit relatively well, hit ground balls to each of the four positions. Fungo hitters that are hitting to the third basemen and shortstops should be bordering the first base line. Fungo hitters hitting to the second and first basemen should be bordering the third base line. Use pitchers or outfielders as ball feeders. Work on straight-on ground balls at first, and once the infielders become comfortable with these, mix in other scenarios: balls hit to the left and right, backhands, line drives, short-hops, pop-ups, and anything in between. Come game time, your infielders will be accustomed to fielding just about everything!

CLEAN FIELDING

Success in this drill depends on fielders starting in a balanced, athletic fielding position and understanding the importance of beating the ball to the spot. Make a line of fielders with one player going at a time from the shortstop position. The coach hits a line drive or groundball at the fielder. If the ball is not fielded cleanly, the player sits out for the remainder of the game. The coach can create a fun, yet pressure-filled situation by saying, "OK, bottom of the ninth and two outs, we're up by one, and you have to make this last out or we lose!" The winner, or last man standing, should receive congratulatory applause from teammates.

CATCHING FLY BALLS

This drill is designed to teach outfielders and infielders how to properly catch fly balls. A coach should first throw an imaginary ball up in the air and instruct fielders to get in correct fly ball catching position. Have them position the glove *between the imaginary ball and their nose.* This will force them to line up the ball so that it comes down directly in the frame of their body. For young fielders afraid of the ball, go from imaginary to tennis or rag balls before using hard balls.

DIRECTIONAL FLY BALLS

This drill gets outfielders accustomed to proper footwork when reacting to balls hit directly over the head, to the left, and to the right. A coach should stand several feet away from an outfielder (the other outfielders at this point are waiting their turn in line). The coach then points which way the outfielder should sprint: back, left, or right. The outfielder must sprint according to the direction in which the coach points. Once the fielder begins his sprint, the coach should throw a fly ball in the direction the player is going. Remind your outfielders never to take their eyes off the ball. For easier fly balls that do not require long runs, fielders should make the catch with two hands and with the glove between the ball and nose. As the drill progresses, the coach should point and throw a fly ball that requires a longer run for the fielder. To make things more competitive, have elimination rounds in which those who miss fly balls are out, and the last remaining outfielder wins the game.

COMMUNICATE

All too often in youth baseball we see routine fly balls turn into extra base hits because of a lack of outfield communication. This drill is designed to foster communication among outfielders. Position outfielders as if it were an actual game — one in left, one in center, and one in right. Coaches should hit ground balls and fly balls in the gaps (in other words, not directly at one fielder, but rather in between two of them) so the outfielders are forced to verbally communicate who will receive the ball. Some coaches prefer their players to yell "you" or "me," or "I got it" or "You got it." If a player is called off, that fielder should assume the backing up role and watch the advancing base runner, letting the other outfielder know where in the infield to throw the ball.

SITUATIONS

This drill is designed to simulate in-game situations. This is as close to an actual game as practice gets! Arrange a team in the field and one up at bat. The "batters" act as runners, since the coach will be hitting the ball in this drill. The coach hits the ball standing on home plate; the runners will start from an area close to home plate. Once contact is made, runners are allowed to advance, reacting to the hit ball. Coaches should purposely create situations, including base hits, fly balls to infielders and outfielders, groundballs, and slow rollers. After three outs, runners should clear the bases. After nine outs, base runners and fielders should switch roles.

FLYING HIGH

For those players who like to fly, this diving drill is ideal! This drill should be used more as a recreational activity than one that hones skills. Coaches yell

"Go!" and either hit or throw balls to fielders just slightly out of their reach. Players will have to run the ball down or, if need be, dive for it. This drill should be done on a softer landing surface so as to not injure the players. Flying high is perfect right before water or break periods.

Drills for Pitching

HIT THE SPOT

It is very important for young pitchers to practice throwing to a target. A good way to practice throwing to a target is to create a game where pitchers get points for throwing to different parts of the catcher. All that is required is a catcher with his equipment on and a pitcher on the mound. The pitcher is awarded points based on the location of the pitch. For instance, throwing a pitch at the catcher's knees might be worth three points, at his chest protector two points, and at his face mask one point. This system emphasizes the importance of keeping the ball down in the strike zone as well as the importance of locating pitches (no points are awarded for velocity). This drill can be turned into a competition, with many pitchers taking turns and the winner being the pitcher throwing the fewest pitches to get to a certain number of points.

THROW A STRIKE

It is very important for young pitchers to have the confidence that they can throw a pitch in a "pressure" situation. To practice this, coaches can have a pitcher enter a game-simulated situation, with the bases loaded, two outs in the last inning, the team up by a run and a 3–2 count on the batter. The pitcher should warm up, and when he is ready, the coach should step into the batter's box and pretend to be a hitter. The coach will not swing at the pitch, however. The pitcher's task is to throw a strike to end the game. This drill is quick, easy to execute, and effective in simulating a pressure situation.

LONG TOSS FOR PITCHERS

It is essential that pitchers develop arm strength at a young age. Long tossing, or extending the typical distance from which players usually throw the baseball, is one way to do this. Pitchers should start 30 feet apart from one another and go through a proper mechanical motion. After each throw, one of the pitchers should take a step back. When the pitchers are a reasonable distance apart (depending on the pitcher, maybe 90 feet), the pitchers should begin awarding points to each other for throwing the ball to different parts of the partner's body. For instance, throwing it to the partner's chest would be worth three points, the head, two points, and anyplace where the partner does not have to move to catch the ball, one point. The first pitcher to reach a designated amount of points (21, for example) wins the game. This game allows pitchers to stretch their arms out while continually emphasizing the importance of throwing to a target. Attempting to hit a target from a longer distance will also make hitting a target from a shorter distance seem easier.

WIFFLE BALL

The development of a young pitcher's arm makes throwing curveballs very dangerous. The stress that a curveball puts on a young pitcher's arm can permanently damage it. But youth pitchers should experiment with grips, stances, and arm angles to throw hitters off. Playing a game of wiffle ball at the end of practice can accomplish just that. Wiffle ball is fun for the entire team, and it creates a competitive setting that is like baseball but is removed enough from the game enough that it will be considered fun, not practice. For pitchers, throwing a wiffle ball is easier because it is lighter. Therefore, coaches do not have to worry about over-extending pitchers' arms. In this way, wiffle ball allows pitchers to practice throwing to a target while experimenting with stances, grips, and arm angles in a game setting but without game-like pressure.

HAVE PITCHERS THROW BATTING PRACTICE

Young pitchers rarely get a chance to pitch to hitters outside of a game situation. Having pitchers throw batting practice is a good opportunity to do just that. By throwing batting practice, pitchers can work on pitches and mechanics without the pressure of working with counts, scores, baserunners, or other game situations.

ARM PATH

The arm path drill is to ensure that the pitcher's entire motion remains in a straight line through the body to the target. Pitchers stand up straight and put their back against a wall. They proceed to go through their motion as if pitching out of the stretch without throwing a ball (although the pitcher should hold a ball as if he was throwing). If the throwing arm touches the wall, the pitcher will know that he has overreached and consequently is likely to have improper mechanics through the remainder of the delivery. Similarly, if the glove or glove arm touches the wall, the pitcher will know that he is not driving his body directly to his intended target.

One Knee

The purpose of the one-knee drill is to emphasize the importance of proper arm path. Pitchers get on one knee (their back knee from the delivery) and slowly over-exaggerate the path of the arm through the motion by dragging the ball along the ground as far back as they can. Then, the pitcher should raise his throwing arm up to the position that it would be in at the point of landing. Finally, from this position, the pitcher should fluidly go through the motion of releasing the ball and then over-exaggerate the follow-through to the outside of the front knee.

Stretch Out

The purpose of the stretch out drill is to familiarize pitchers with the point at which the body should be when the ball is released. Pitchers get to the point where the front leg is planted as it would be right before the pitch, with the torso in an upright position, the front arm pointed at the target, and the throwing arm in the highest point of its path. It is important that the pitcher stretch out the front leg as far as possible (as the name suggests) to emphasize the importance of driving the body to the target. The pitcher then torques through his delivery, over-exaggerating the follow-through.

Balance Point

The purpose of the balance point drill is to emphasize how important it is to reach this point and be able to hold it in a strong and erect position. Pitchers go through their motion and reach the point at which their leg is at the apex of its lift. This is balance point. Balance point should be held for a count of five, followed by the rest of the delivery.

BALANCE BEAM

The purpose of the balance beam drill is to ensure that pitchers are driving directly to the target. Incorporating an aspect of the balance point drill, pitchers should stand on a balance beam, reach balance point and hold for a count of five. Then the pitcher should continue the rest of his motion, which should result in the front foot planting on the balance beam. This beam should be a six- to eight-inch wide piece of wood. If the pitcher does not plant on the balance beam, it means that he is not driving towards the target with all of his energy. The balance beam drill can also be used to mark how far the pitcher is striding.

TOWEL WHIP

The purpose of the towel whip drill is to emphasize to pitchers the importance of the follow-through by creating a drill that requires them to reach out and follow all the way through the delivery, finishing with a flat back and low to the ground. Pitchers should get into the position from the stretch out drill, with the body in the landing position from the pitching motion. Instead of a ball in the throwing hand, the pitcher holds a towel. This drill requires a partner kneeling approximately five or six feet away from the pitcher when in the stretch out position. This partner should be extending a glove away from his body. The pitcher should go through his motion from stretch out point and try to whip the glove with the towel. The only way it should be possible to hit the glove is with a full and exaggerated follow-through.

Appendix Two:
Practice Games

SOFT-TOSS SCRIMMAGE

Treat this as a regular scrimmage, but instead of live pitches, you should throw soft-toss to the hitters. Feel free to tweak the game to include intense game-like situations, such as placing a runner at third base with one out.

TWO-PITCH GAMES

During a regular scrimmage, restrict batters to having only two pitches to hit the ball. Taking a strike and fouling a ball off both count as pitches. Having only two pitches will simulate the pressure of real games. Also, as a hustle drill, give only 30 seconds for the teams to change sides from offense to defense.

HITTING THE OPPOSITE WAY

In a manner similar to the game that pulled in each of the foul lines, hold practice scrimmages where batters must hit the opposite way so that one foul line runs up the middle of the field. The pitcher should try to pitch to the outside half of the plate.

FREEZE

This game encourages heads-up, aggressive baserunning. The team is divided into hitters and fielders, as in a regular scrimmage. However, each player is playing for himself and keeps track of the number runs he scores. When a player reaches base, he can try to take the next base any time he wants to. However, if he is off a base at any time the pitcher (coach) is holding the ball on the mound, he is out. Furthermore, more than one player can occupy the same base at any given time. (It gets a bit comical when there are three or more players on one base.) Fielders try to get balls quickly back to the pitcher, who is standing on the mound.

OLYMPICS

This practice game emphasizes both speed on the basepaths and taking a proper banana path. Divide the team into two teams with one starting at home plate (team A) and the other starting at second base (team B). At your signal, one player from each team takes off, team A to second base and team B to home. The next player in line starts off only when his teammate has reached second (team A) or home (team B). The first team to finish wins the game. Be careful to have players arranged so they do not collide.

2–1 COUNT SCRIMMAGE

As your season progresses, you can shape your practices to mirror game experiences, all while stressing proper fundamentals among your players. One easy way to do this is through a "2–1 Count Scrimmage." You treat this like a regular scrimmage during practice, with a pitcher throwing to your players. However, unlike a regular game, you shape it so that each batter starts off with a 2–1 count. This is designed to speed up the pace of a normal scrimmage and put pressure on the pitcher to throw strikes and the hitter to swing. There is little room for error with a 2–1 count, on the part of both the pitcher and the hitter. The hitter is forced to go up to the plate with the attitude that he will have to swing the bat, just like you would like them to approach an at-bat in a game. The pitcher, meanwhile, takes the mound with the perception that throwing a first-pitch strike is the most important thing to do.

GOING OPPOSITE

This practice game is designed to practice the important skill of hitting the outside pitch to the opposite field. For righties, this means right field, and for lefties, it means left field. Coaches should set up a series of cones or objects in a line directly through the middle of the field, stretching all the way to deep center. All of the fielders should be scattered throughout right field (for righties) or left (for lefties). Like a normal batting practice, the coach will be pitching to a player who is assuming his normal stance at home plate. However, it should be each player's goal to hit every pitch the other way (opposite field). Preferably, the coach should attempt to throw balls middle of the plate and away, with the intention of reinforcing the need to "stay back and drive the ball the other way." To add excitement, especially for younger players, make hard grounders worth one point, long fly balls worth two, and line drives worth three. Then compete to see who can rack up the most points.

STICKBALL

This practice game is modeled after the popular playground game. Each player will take his turn at the plate, and the rest of the team will be out in the field while the coach pitches. There is no running the bases. Each player should get approximately ten strikes. Grounders fielded cleanly and any ball caught on a fly are an out. Grounders that are not caught and lazy fly balls that are not caught are a single. Any line drive through the infield is a double, as is a "normal" fly ball that is not caught. Triples include line drives into the outfield, and any balls rolling far past the outfielders. Any ball over the fence or on a fly (or line) over everyone's head is a homer. "Pretend" runners, or ghost runners, will be running the bases. Each player gets three outs, and whoever has the most runs at the end is the winner.

FREEZE

This practice game is designed to be an all-inclusive version of batting practice. Two groups are assembled, one in the field and one at-bat. However, each individual player will be trying to score as many points as possible for himself. The coach will pitch, and players will hit as usual, reaching base if their hit is not fielded cleanly. The difference here is that a player will be called out if he is off any of the three bases while the coach has the ball on the pitcher's mound. Therefore, the object of the fielders is to get the ball to the coach as soon as possible. Once they reach base, players advance at their own risk, usually when the ball is hit far away from the coach or there is an overthrow to the coach. It is permissible for more than one player to occupy the same "base area" at any time. This drill gets interesting when four or five players are all on second at the same time. Outs are recorded when a player strikes out, or a ball is caught on the fly. Each player tries to score as many runs as possible, and each team gets three outs per inning.

SITUATIONS

This practice game is designed to simulate in-game situations. There will be one batter at a time, one catcher, and the rest of the team in the field. It is simple yet effective because players can get a taste of in-game pressures and success. The coach will pitch and create the situation, such as "One out, tying run on third—you gotta get him in!" or "No outs, man on second—you gotta get him to third base!" or "No outs, man on first—bunt him over!" Then, after giving the hitter the situation and objectives, points can be awarded depending on the outcome of his at-bat. For example, award five points for a sac fly, 10 points for a line drive base hit, or three points for a bloop base hit, 10 for a sac bunt, five for successfully moving the runner from second to third by hitting the ball to right field, etc. Play until each player gets equal chances to hit, and see who has the most points.

BUNT SCRIMMAGE

This drill shapes the game to work on bunt defense and bunt offense, allowing only bunts to be executed on offense. Sparingly place runners on base to cause different shifts in the defense and different bunts to be performed at the plate.

BASEBALL FOOTBALL

Divide your team into two squads and set up a "football field" using cones in the outfield. As the coach, you are the permanent quarterback. All players should have their gloves, and the game is played just like regular football—two-hand touch—but with baseballs and gloves.

Appendix Three: Resources

Books

American Sport Education Program. *Coaching Youth Baseball*. Champaign, IL: Human Kinetics, 1996.

Bennett, Bob (ed.). *The Baseball Drill Book*. Champaign, IL: Human Kinetics, 2004.

Bigelow, Bob, Tom Moroney, and Linda Hall. *Just Let the Kids Play*. Deerfield Beach, FL: Health Communications, 2001.

Carroll, Beverly, Kevin O'Brien, and Fran O'Brien. *How to Coach Youth Baseball: A Step-by-Step Approach*. Guilford, CT: Lyons Press, 2007.

Coakley, Jay. *Sport in Society: Issues and Controversies*. New York: McGraw-Hill, 1998.

Curran, Mike. *Coaching Baseball Successfully*. Champaign, IL: Human Kinetics, 2007.

Devereux, Edward. "Backyard Versus Little League Baseball: The Impoverishment of Children's Games." In Rainers Martins (ed.), *Joy and Sadness in Children's Sports*. Champaign, IL: Human Kinetics, 1978.

Doyle, Daniel, and Deborah Burch. *The Encyclopedia of Sports Parenting*. Kingston, RI: Hall of Fame Press, 2008.

Fine, Gary. *With the Boys: Little League Baseball and Preadolescent Culture*. Chicago: University of Chicago Press, 1987.

Gallagher, Dave, and Mark Gola. *The Little League Hitter's Journal*. New York: McGraw-Hill, 2005.

Gola, Mark. *Coaching the Little League Fielder*. New York: McGraw-Hill, 2005.

_____. *The Little League Guide to Conditioning and Training: Preparing Young Players with Fundamentals and Basics*. New York: McGraw-Hill, 2004.

_____, and John Monteleone. *The Complete Book of Hitting Faults and Fixes*. New York: McGraw-Hill, 2001.

Hanlon, Tom. *Absolute Beginner's Guide to Coaching Youth Baseball*. Indianapolis: Que Publishing, 2005.

Launder, Alan. *Play Practice: The Games Approach to Teaching and Coaching Sports*. Champaign, IL: Human Kinetics, 2001.

Martens, Rainer. *Successful Coaching*. Champaign, IL: Human Kinetics, 2004.

McIntosh, Ned. *Managing Little League Baseball*. New York: McGraw-Hill, 2008.

Monteleone, John. *Coaching the Little League Hitter*. New York: McGraw-Hill, 2004.

_____. *The Little League Guide to Correcting the 25 Most Common Mistakes*. Chicago: Contemporary Books, 2003.

Myers, Doug, and Mark Gola. *The Complete Book of Pitching*. Chicago: Contemporary Books, 2000.

Nucci, Larry. *Education in the Moral Domain*. Cambridge, U.K.: Cambridge University Press, 2001.

O'Connell, Tom. *Coaching Baseball: Technical and Tactical Skills*. Champaign, IL: Human Kinetics, 2005.

Omli, Jens, and Nicole LaVoi. "Background Anger in Youth Sport: A Perfect Storm?" Paper presented at the Association for Moral Education, 2008.

Ripken, Cal, Jr. *Coaching Youth Baseball the Ripken Way*. Champaign, IL: Human Kinetics, 2007.

Rivkin, Mary. *The Great Outdoors: Restoring Children's Right to Play Outside*. Washington, D.C.: National Association for the Education of Young Children, 1995.

Schupak, Marty. *Youth Baseball Drills*. Champaign, IL: Human Kinetics, 2005.

Seefeldt, Vern, Martha Ewing, and Stephan Walk. *Overview of Youth Sports Programs in the United States*. Washington, D.C.: Carnegie Council on Adolescent Development, 1992.

Smith, Ronald Edward. *Way to Go Coach: A Scientifically-Proven Approach to Coaching Effectiveness*. Portola Valley, CA: Warde Publishers, 1995.

Thompson, Jim. *The Double Goal Coach: Positive Coaching Tools for Honoring the Game and Developing Winners in Sports and Life*. New York: HarperCollins, 2003.

Thurston, Bill. *Coaching Youth Baseball: A Baffled Parents Guide*. Camden, ME: Ragged Mountain Press, 2000.

Tocco, Amy. *Coaching Youth Baseball (Coaching Youth Sports)*. Champaign, IL: Human Kinetics, 2007.

Wiggins, David. "A History of Highly Competitive Sport for American Children." In Frank Smoll and Ronald Edward Smith (eds.), *Children and Youth in Sport: A Biopsychosocial Perspective*. New York: McGraw-Hill, 1996.

Winkin, John, Joy Kemble, and Michael Coutts. *Maximizing Baseball Practice*. Champaign, IL: Human Kinetics, 1995.

Websites

Drills for Practice

http://www.eteamz.com/baseball/instruction/tips/
www.juniorbaseball.com
www.youthbaseballbasics.com/coaching.shtml
http://www.baseballdrills.info
http://www.webball.com/cms/page1143.cfm
http://www.leaguelineup.com/coachingtips.asp
http://www.hit2win.com/coachdrills.html
www.43drills.com
www.coachingtball.com
http://www.sportspracticedrills.com/Category/Baseball/50

Tips for Becoming a Positive Coach

www.qcbaseball.com
www.responsiblesports.com
www.y-coach.com
www.nays.org/onlinepromo/onlinehome.html
www.positivecoach.org
www.alandalbaseball.com
www.amateurbaseballcoaching.com
http://www.baseballideas.blogspot.com
http://youthbaseball_e_zine.homestead.com
http://www.bagsbaseball.com/coachswp.htm
http://www.bettercoaches.com/home/index.htm

Links to the Homepages of Youth Leagues in America
(Providers of rules, locations of leagues, etc.)

www.aaubaseball.org
www.aabc.us
www.baberuthbaseball.org
www.cababaseball.com
www.dixie.org
www.dizzydeanbbinc.org
www.hapdumontbaseball.com
www.nabf.com
www.nationalpal.org
www.pony.org
www.teeballusa.org

Equipment

www.baseballexpress.com
www.sportsauthority.com
www.baseballsavings.com
www.baseballwarehouse.com
www.baseballtips.com

Issues for Coaches

www.y-coach.com/forums.html
www.thecoachingstore.com/articles/default.html
www.youthbaseballinfo.com/index.php
www.baseball-fever.com
http://www.baseball-rules.com/FAQs.htm
http://www.eteamz.com/austinareaponyball/news/index.cfm?cat=217584
http://www.i70clinic.com
http://teachkidsbaseball.com

Videos

The Charley Lau Art of Hitting .300 (2002)
The 59 Minute Baseball Practice (1999)
The 150 Baseball Drills, Games and Activities for Kids (3 DVD Set) (2008)
Baseball Skills & Drills (2005)

Index

Index